DAVID SMITH

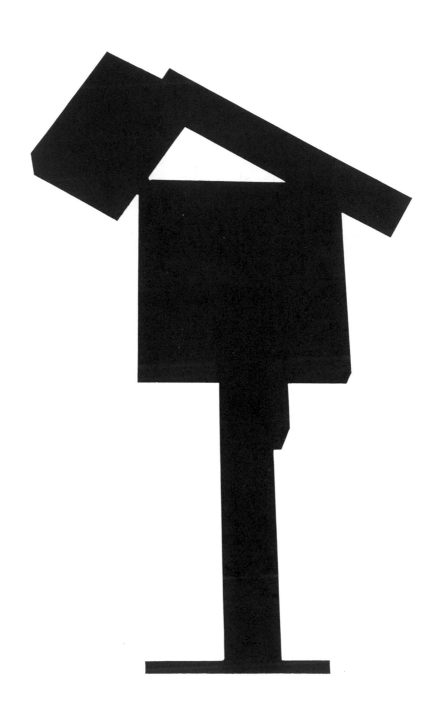

DAVID SMITH

The Sculptor and His Work

STANLEY E. MARCUS

Cornell University Press ITHACA AND LONDON

All photographs by David Smith on deposit in David Smith papers at the Archives of American Art, Smithsonian Institution, Washington, D.C., copyright Candida and Rebecca Smith.

Cornell University Press gratefully acknowledges a grant from the Andrew W. Mellon Foundation that aided in bringing this book to publication.

First published 1983 by Cornell University Press.
Published in the United Kingdom by Cornell University Press Ltd., London.

International Standard Book Number 0-8014-1510-1
Library of Congress Catalog Card Number 83-45148
Printed in the United States of America
Librarians: Library of Congress cataloging information appears on the last page of the book.

The paper in this book is acid-free and meets the guidelines for permanence and durability of the Committee on Production Guidelines for Book Longevity of the Council on Library Resources.

For Rebecca and the children

CONTENTS

ILLUSTRATIONS

PREFACE

Over the course of a twenty-year career, David Smith produced a prodigious number of sculptures in a great diversity of styles. His development was not methodical. Abrupt changes came seemingly without reference to previous directions. To understand what was happening and why, one must look beyond the works and into Smith's life. My purpose is to offer an assessment of Smith's sculptural oeuvre, not to write his biography, yet it is impossible to understand the particular directions he took unless we examine the experiences that led to his choices. Those aspects of Smith's personality which directly affect his work also require examination. Some of the reminiscences of his friends and associates which help to illuminate that personality provide personal glimpses also of a period that is undoubtedly one of the most vital in the history of American art, the 1940s and 1950s.

Source materials on David Smith's life are scarce. Smith himself offered little information about himself in his writings or in conversation with his friends. Much of what he did offer was inaccurate or distorted. It appears that Smith intended to create a legend about himself, and he succeeded. The primary documentation of his life and his work is found in the Archives of American Art in Washington, D.C. At the time of Smith's death, much material was gathered from files at Bolton Landing, New York, where he had his workshop. Some seven to eight thousand documents were placed on microfilm; several additional boxes of invoices and unassorted papers remain unfilmed. By piecing these papers together, I could trace much of Smith's career. Coupled with my own knowledge as a sculptor of welded metals, these materials have enabled me to see Smith's work in a light quite different from the one to which earlier studies have accustomed us.

Those studies have focused largely on Smith's imagery, a facet of his work which I think ought not to be of primary concern. I see greater importance in the development of Smith's forms, particularly in view of the hitherto relatively unexplored medium that he was using. I do not deny the importance as well as the interest of his imagery, particularly in his early works. Still, those works have had little influence on succeeding generations of sculptors, perhaps because they are so personal. By contrast, welding is now taught in nearly all art schools in the United States, a development directly attributable to Smith. The way his forms evolved should be a matter of great significance to today's sculptors and to others who are curious about the consequences of using a new art form. The opportunity to make sculptures of large scale and limited cost has proved irresistible to sculptors everywhere.

Smith's invention of a new vocabulary of structure and form is still viable, twenty-five years later. His terms are not arbitrary, but derived from the nature of the medium and the technique. His new idiom was developed through painful trial and error, and by tracing that development we can gain insight into the ramifications of radical innovation. The widespread adoption of Smith's innovation makes such an attempt obligatory. Smith struggled for over fifteen years to find a satisfactory way of realizing his new art form and spent another fifteen years in its elaboration and exploitation. This book attempts to tell of those struggles and of the development of Smith's art.

There are many people whom I thank for their assistance. Dorothy Dehner gave many hours graciously. Jean Freas Pond helped me to see elements of Smith's symbolism. Leon Arkus, Herman Cherry, Didi Croll at the Archives of American Art, Lloyd Goodrich, Garnett McCoy, the late Leon Pratt, Barbara Salazar, Robert Turner, librarian at the University of Texas of the Permian Basin, and Marian Willard have also been very helpful. To Clement Greenberg I owe a special debt of gratitude for his encouragement and advice. His enthusiasm for this book has been very rewarding to me. I also thank Rebecca and Candida Smith for the privilege of using the material in the Archives of American Art and Daniel Snodderly and the staff at Cornell University Press.

STANLEY E. MARCUS

Odessa, Texas

DAVID SMITH

1

AN OVERVIEW OF
SMITH'S ART

Traditionally, sculptors have based their art on the human figure, with emphasis on the masses of head and torso. When some sculptors began to work in abstract forms in the early twentieth century, they had no logical need to continue to emphasize mass, yet the preoccupation with mass continued, directed now toward the making of "objects." The quintessence of objectification was achieved in Constantin Brancusi's egglike forms, in which nothing distracted from the solidity of the masses. Brancusi's influence continued to dominate American sculpture in the 1930s, as can be seen in the tightly packed, curvilinear forms of William Zorach and José de Creeft, the bulbous ones of Elie Nadelman, and the rocklike sculptures of John Flannagan. Paul Manship's elegant bronzes were concerned with space as well as form, but their rigid stylization kept them as frozen as the object forms of the stone carvers. Nothing sums up the feeling of the period more succinctly than Mahonri Young's *Stevedore*, a plodding figure bent under the massive burden on his head.

Limitations were placed not only on form but on material as well. Traditionally, sculptors seemed determined to compete in fluency with the masters of the pencil and looked for mediums just as responsive to their control. They sought durability too, perhaps to compensate for the time and effort expended on their work. Sculpture was expected to last many generations, creating a sense of awe and veneration, as either a relic of the past or a gift to the future. Even today "object" sculpture is sometimes used to inspire a sense of sublimity. Such works make ideal monuments and symbols because their simple contours are easily remembered. The marble and bronze of which they are made have become honored by their long association with the noble purposes of sculpture, to the point where their use alone sometimes suffices to cause objects made from stone or bronze to be considered works of art.

The first major American challenge to the supremacy of massed form, or monolithism, was made by David Smith. Through the repeated use of modular steel forms fabricated in factories he negated the importance of unique form as the sole criterion for judging sculpture. The idiosyncratic object was replaced by an art of spaces. The physical hollowness of the forms he used was a further rebuttal to the claims to supremacy of the solid object.

Smith's achievements in the use of space stem from his systematic exploration of welding, a technique he was almost alone in using. Pablo Picasso, with Julio Gonzalez doing the welding, had constructed several welded works in 1928 and 1929. Smith saw a reproduction of one and realized the potential of welding as a means of working metal directly into sculptural form. After his collaboration with Picasso, Gonzalez went on to weld sculptures of his own. While his forms moved into space in a manner unique to sculpture, they remained essentially monolithic. Smith, however, was concerned from the beginning with spatial environments and interaction among forms. At the start of his career as a sculptor, in the mid-1930s, his interacting forms were little more than figures on a stage. Smith seemed intent on reconciling space with forms found in nature; the wire he used to simulate penciled lines enabled the eye to penetrate the forms. By the mid-1940s he had switched completely to figurative work, using a somewhat heavy-handed symbolism. Those solid-cored works, anticipated by the 1938–40 *Medals for Dishonor,* involved little welding; they were done in a variety of techniques, some of which were quite complex. Significantly, during this period Smith found it necessary to cast some of his objects in the manner of traditional sculptors in order to achieve the highly mimetic forms he desired. (Wax, the most widely used preliminary material in the casting process, is highly malleable and, consequently, very responsive to the shaping of intricate forms.)

In 1950 Smith's ideas changed radically. Using "found objects" from industrial detritus he returned to welding as his basic technique. He began to strip his forms of their symbolic and figurative trappings as he became increasingly concerned with forms as they existed in space. It is not coincidence that during this period Smith and the painters known as the "New York Group" explored similar problems of structure and space. Smith knew those painters personally. In part because of his painter's background, he had never accepted the traditional separation of pictorial and sculptural approaches; "pictorially," he came to adopt the frontal plane in preference to sculpture in the round. Recognizing the compositional issues developed by the New York Group, Smith applied them to sculpture. By the early 1950s, Smith had adopted the New York painters' idea of removing the focal area from the center of the composition and transferring elements closer to the periphery, as in his *Hudson River Landscape* (Fig. 1) of 1951. He began systematically to exploit his open frameworks and in the process subverted the monolithic block's domination of sculpture.

Picasso had set the precedent with his 1912 *Guitar* construction, developing a system of planes as an outgrowth of experiments with collage. His 1909 effort, in the bust of Fernande Olivier, to construct a system of planes had failed because the monolithic form remained intact. The planes were reduced to a superficial surface treatment. He handled them in much the same way he did the forms in his Analytical Cubist paintings, which were equally bound to objects. Collage taught Picasso to concentrate not on the object but on the arrangement of shapes on a common ground. This idea was carried over into *Guitar,* in which the guitar's contour locks together a variety of unrelated shapes.

For many years Smith's work was not well received. The strangely flattened format and the tension produced by unidentifiable forms scattered in space seemed unaesthetic in comparison with the continuous skin and curving lines that could make monolithic form so blandly pleasant. His material was harsh steel. The viewer was confronted rather than

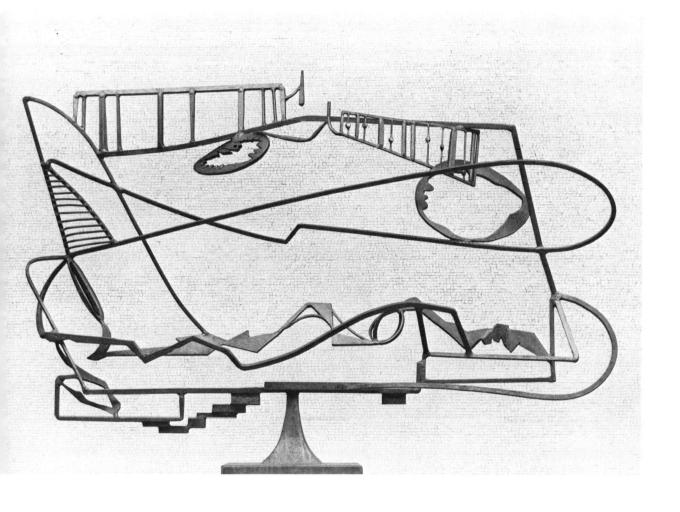

Fig. 1. *Hudson River Landscape,* 1951. Steel. 49½ × 75 × 16¾″. Collection and photo courtesy Whitney Museum of American Art, New York. Photo by Geoffrey Clements

soothed. Smith's most difficult task was to recognize and eliminate assumptions based on monolithic traditions, just as Picasso had had to do earlier. Smith did not fully grasp the close association between the human figure and the monolith until he was close to the end of his career. The welding torch is ill suited to the modeling of organic forms, imparting an awkwardness to them.

A particular problem for Smith was his idea of "concept," a vague notion that combined the general direction of an artist's development with the intent of the particular work to be made. He was governed for many years by the belief that neither material nor technique ought to influence purpose in the making of a sculpture. This nineteenth-century attitude was workable when the material and technique were known quantities. When the medium and technique were relatively new, preconceived ideas ("concepts") would only hamper their possibilities by deterring experimentation. Smith had built an early reputation on his novel technique. It was many years before his art became acceptable for itself. His concern over the priority of "concept" reflected this struggle to achieve recognition as an artist rather than as an eccentric craftsman.

The question arises as to why Smith, as a tyro, would choose a medium, welded steel, completely unsuited to traditional sculptural values, and then persist in the face of discouragement by critics and apathy among museum directors and gallery owners. The hardness of steel makes it difficult to work and to buff. Its high melting point and low viscosity make it difficult to cast. Low cost is of advantage only when the volume of production is large; it offers no benefits in a field where exclusivity is so important that it is extended to the material, as in the case of marble and bronze. Nor were steel's utilitarian associations likely to be of advantage in an area where notions of eliteness prevailed. Least desirable is the vulnerability of mild steel to rust—and rust is associated with the detritus of civilization, not with its ideals. While Smith was unquestionably attracted to the possibilities that welding offered for movement into space, it still seems unusual that an inexperienced sculptor should have chosen a medium neglected by more knowledgeable artists. The explanation may well lie in emotional factors.

The welding of steel may have filled a psychological need in Smith. He had been raised in the Midwest and steeped in its work ethic. That same ethic tended to reduce art to the status of a pastime for women. By using factory methods to make sculpture, Smith may have been seeking masculine associations. Men who work in steel are identified with its toughness and strength. Smith took pride in his having worked with such men, and in their acceptance of him. He exaggerated his factory experience to make himself appear to be a blue-collar worker turned artist. All the same, Smith was capable in the use of industrial tools, comfortable with them. From childhood he had been taught about machinery. His pleasure was derived from researching and mastering new techniques.

Yet the materials and techniques of industry were not then associated with the making of art. Smith's particular talents were alien to Midwestern concepts about art and artists. From early childhood he had absorbed the notion that artists were "ethereal" beings with gifts of talent that bordered on the divine. It seemed improbable that such persons were likely to be found in a rough rural environment. Smith's efforts to draw the figure, though vigorous, were heavy and awkward and would remain so. Smith also had difficulty in handling color. Thus he seemed unexceptional in those skills that were thought essential to making art. In traditional modes, Smith's skills would not have taken him far. In part, the recognition of his limitations must have been what finally persuaded him, after many years, to abandon his attempts to become a painter and to do what he knew best—work with machinery. The use of steel, a coarse, hard material, seemed inappropriate for art. And the work was not produced in a comfortable atelier but in a dirty workshop in the rigorous climate of Bolton Landing, New York, on the western shore of Lake George. It should not be surprising that Smith's awkward early work was not welcomed by art dealers.

The choice of a medium shunned by more facile artists left Smith in isolation and increasingly angry at the rejection he felt. Even the materials of traditional art became targets for his anger. "What do you want from bronze—to perpetuate the ruling class idols—that if its bronze its art."[1]

Smith's hostility and chafing at restrictive rules enabled him to reject those artistic traditions that were beyond his reach. Rejection of authority and regulations was traceable back to Smith's childhood. It was his mother who conveyed to Smith the standard notions about art, what it was, what it ought to be. A schoolteacher who throughout her life was deeply concerned with respectability, she made strenuous efforts to ensure that David would conform to her values. Anger he had felt since childhood at what he perceived as smothering authority was expanded in adulthood to include institutions that he saw as authoritarian—most particularly the Museum of Modern Art in New York and Alfred Barr, its first director, whose judgments seemed to determine quality in modern art (though Smith's feeling toward that institution was not unique among his generation of artists). Under the guise of moral indignation, Smith's *Medals for Dishonor* indiscriminately lump together the Ku Klux Klan, the German-American Bund, the clergy, the Nazis, the New Deal, the rich, and doctors.

Yet underneath the rage was a desire to belong and a strong feeling of isolation. When Smith eventually began to accept his success, his attitude, even toward the Modern, underwent significant change. It could be seen in Smith's work. A lyricism in the late sculptures replaced the uneven, bristly quality of the early ones, just as the rusted mild steel itself was increasingly replaced by the gleaming surfaces of stainless steel.

2

STARTING OUT

David Smith arrived in New York City by way of Washington, D.C., in the summer of 1926 when he was twenty years old. His forebears had left Culpepper County, Virginia, to settle in Decatur, Indiana, where his grandfather donated land for the courthouse. It was here that Smith was born and lived until 1921, when the family moved to Paulding, Ohio.

His father, Harvey, was something of an inventor and a small-scale businessman, who eventually became part-owner of a telephone company. Reserved in demeanor, he maintained a cordial though formal relationship with his son. David's mother, Golda, combined her interest in education with considerable concern for cultural matters and a deep devotion to the Methodist church. She expected her son to share that devotion. Church attendance on Sunday was mandatory, and dancing, gambling, drinking, and discussion of sex were forbidden. Though money was scarce, sums were regularly laid aside for his college education, with the expectation that he would train to become either a schoolteacher or a stenographer.

Smith grew up resenting the constraints put upon him. Of his education he later wrote, "In childhood we have been raped by word pictures. We must revolt against all word authority."[1] Although there is no evidence to indicate a particularly deprived childhood, he later remembered with bitterness having to work in a candy kitchen and to clean celery on Saturday mornings when his friends were at play. A source of comfort and refuge was his grandmother Catherine Stoler, his mother's mother. It was at the back of her Bible that Smith saw the photographs of Egypt which were to foster a lifetime interest in Egyptian culture and hieroglyphs, as well as in art in general.

At Paulding High School Smith was an indifferent student, although he received A's and B's in art. He drew the illustrations for the school yearbook. In 1923 he took a cartoon correspondence course from the Cleveland Art School and henceforth was known as "Bud," after Bud Fisher, creator of the comic strip "Mutt and Jeff." From his father Smith acquired a familiarity with explosives and machinery. As high school pranks he fired off the cannon in the town square and exploded dynamite in the fields. Smith again used firearms to vent his anger later in Washington, D.C., where, before leaving a short-lived bank job, he emptied the magazine of a pistol into the floor.

In 1924 Smith enrolled at Ohio University. He stayed only a year. He later claimed that his reason for leaving was the poor quality of art instruction. But his grades in art courses were good—it was in other areas of instruction that he either failed or barely passed.[2] During the summer of 1925 he went to work at the Studebaker automobile factory in South Bend, Indiana. That was his only factory experience before World War II. The assembly line had not yet been introduced and each worker was expected to perform a wide variety of tasks, including riveting, drilling, lathe work, milling, and spot welding. However, Smith did not finally learn to weld with the oxyacetylene torch, a factory process that he turned into a widely imitated art technique, until his association with the workers at the Terminal Iron Works in Brooklyn, New York, in 1933—though he had begun to experiment with the torch the year before.

On the basis of his summer at South Bend, Smith created the myth that he had been a welder and steelworker before becoming a sculptor. The factory experience had a lasting effect and was the source of many ideas later incorporated in his shop at Bolton Landing. "In work progress I control the entire process from origin to finish. There are no in-between craftsmen or process distortions. It is the complete and total processing of the work of art."[3] The industrial process fascinated him: "The association of steel retained steel function of shapes moving and circumscribing upon axis, moving and gearing against each other at different speeds as the association of this metal suggests."[4]

In the fall of 1925 Smith returned to school, this time the University of Notre Dame. It is not certain whether or not he completed the semester. Late 1925 or early 1926 found him at the Studebaker Finance Agency, which soon transferred him to Washington, D.C. From there he went to the Morris Plan Bank, from which he soon departed in the violent way described above.[5]

Sometime during that first New York summer of 1926, Smith's landlord gave him the name of a young art student living in the same building who she thought might help Smith in his art career. That student, Dorothy Dehner, suggested that he study at the Art Students' League, where she herself was taking courses. Smith enrolled that fall and studied with Richard Lahey at night while he worked days at the Industrial Acceptance Corporation, next door to the Art Students' League. The following year, 1927, Smith studied with John Sloan. On December 24, he and Dorothy Dehner were married.

Dorothy's cultural background was considerably different from Smith's. His exposure to arts had hitherto been limited to reproductions. According to Smith's own account, it was commonly believed in Decatur that the creative process was restricted to an inspired few, of whom Smith was presumably not one.[6] For Dorothy Dehner, art and life were intertwined. Her mother had been interested in dance, and an aunt with whom she lived after her mother's death had graduated from the Cincinnati Conservatory of Music. Raised on the West Coast, she early became interested in the theater and had worked at the Pasadena Playhouse. By the time she met David Smith, Dorothy Dehner had been to Europe and had seen there works of Picasso, Matisse, and Giacometti, among others. Originally interested in sculpture, she had viewed William Zorach's class at the Art Students' League. Finding

Zorach too traditional, she began to study drawing with Kimon Nicolaides. It is not surprising that for many years Dorothy Dehner served as an informal tutor to Smith, guiding his taste in art and literature.

Though the marriage was essentially happy in the early years, within the first month the violent side of Smith's nature surfaced. When he accidentally spilled some milk on the table one day, Dorothy gave an exclamation of surprise. Smith picked up the tablecloth with everything on it and hurled it against the wall. He then ran out and threw himself into the icy Hudson River, from which he was fished by two boatmen. Returning in frozen clothing to his agitated wife, he had an explanation: "See what you made me do!"[7] Those spells of anger became more frequent in time. And he remained vulnerable to criticism, whether real or imagined.

Shortly after his marriage, Smith wrote a series of letters to Florence Uphof (Figs. 2, 3, and 4), one of the two maiden aunts who had raised Dorothy. Those letters reveal much about his youthful personality. They show a need for mothering, all the more interesting in view of the fact that Smith had not yet met Miss Uphof. The lofty ambitions, and also the meticulous accounting of funds, in the letters are early manifestations of later traits. What would disappear was the exuberance. With charming naivety, Smith expressed the wonders of being free, young, and in New York, working at a career that interested him. The joy did not last. The exuberance became transformed into a drive whose goal was nothing less than recognition as the best sculptor in America. To Smith there was a simple way to have that decided: whoever received the highest prices became the best. (Later on, he kept a wary eye on competitors, particularly on Jacques Lipchitz, and got enormous satisfaction when one of his exhibitions did better in sales.)

Much of the Smiths' early social and artistic life centered around the teachers, administrators, and students at the Art Students' League. Smith was interested in recent European movements. When John Sloan called Cubism "assembly-line art,"[8] Smith switched from Sloan's class to Jan Matulka's, though he continued to respect Sloan.

In 1928, after his painting course failed to attract the minimum enrollment, Matulka met with students privately in a small second-floor loft on Fourteenth Street. Along with Smith were I. Rice Pereira, Burgoyne Diller, George MacNeil, Edgar Levy, and Lucille Corcos (who later married Levy). The group became good friends and both Smiths became particularly close to the Levys. During the summer of 1929 the Smiths (Fig. 5) spent several weeks as paying guests of Thomas and Weber Furlong, respectively treasurer and executive secretary of the Art Students' League, at the Furlongs' farm above Bolton Landing, New York. During that visit they had many long discussions of art, with particular emphasis on Cubism, which Furlong had studied with Max Weber. Evidently it was an enjoyable visit: Smith decided to stay an additional month, taking leave from A. G. Spalding, the sporting-goods house where he was employed as "director of accommodations" (he had chosen the title himself).

While visiting the Furlongs, the Smiths decided to seek a weekend place for themselves, and they spent considerable time searching for a house with a view. Dorothy had a small income from her mother's estate, and if they did not aim too high, they might be able to

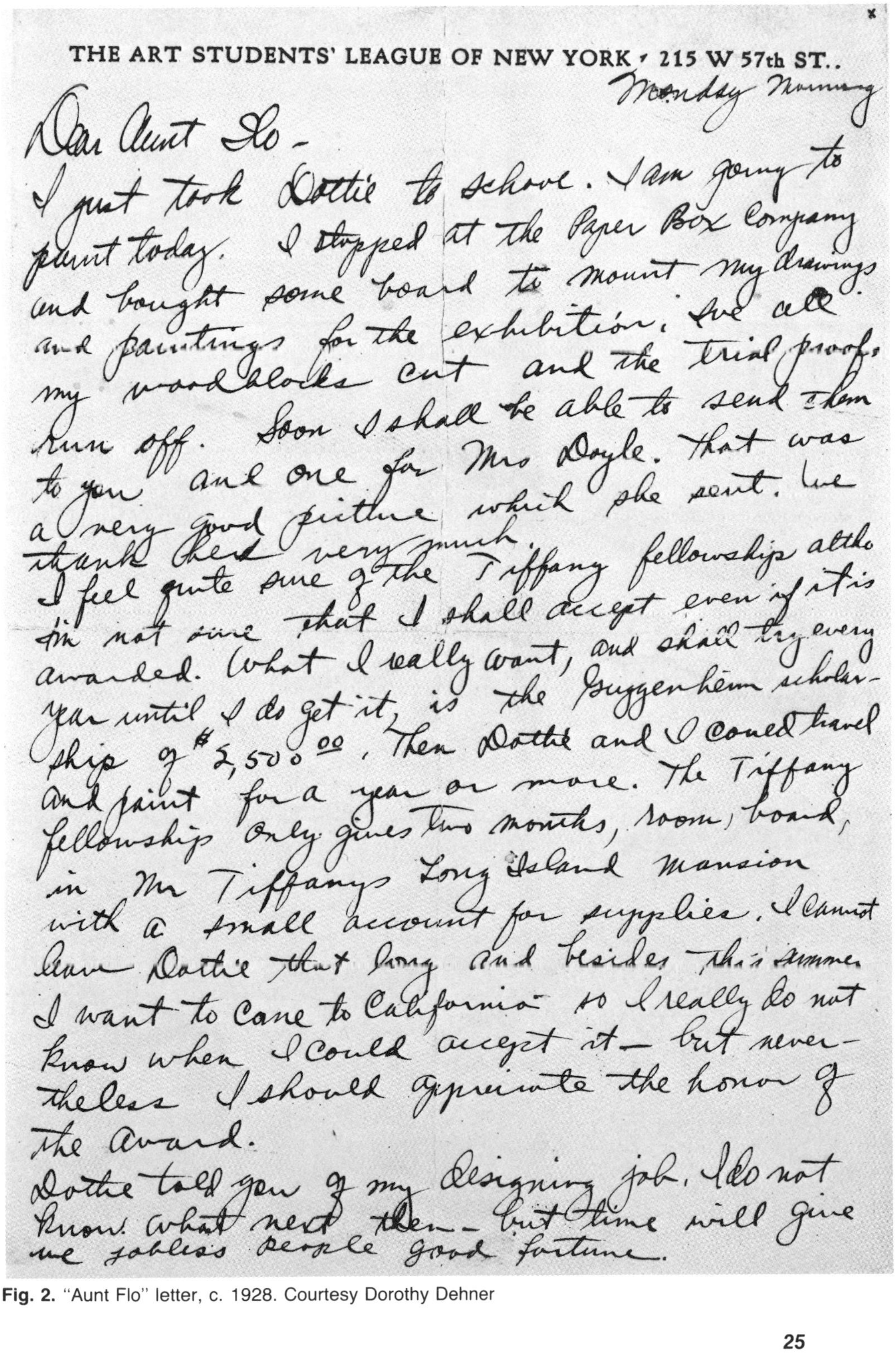

THE ART STUDENTS' LEAGUE OF NEW YORK · 215 W 57th ST..

Monday Morning

Dear Aunt Flo -

I just took Dottie to school. I am going to paint today. I stopped at the Paper Box Company and bought some board to mount my drawings and paintings for the exhibition. I've all my woodblocks cut and the trial proofs run off. Soon I shall be able to send them to you and one for Mrs Doyle. That was a very good picture which she sent. We thank her very much.

I feel quite sure of the Tiffany fellowship altho I'm not sure that I shall accept even if it is awarded. What I really want, and shall try every year until I do get it, is the Guggenheim scholarship of $2,500.00. Then Dottie and I could travel and paint for a year or more. The Tiffany fellowship only gives two months, room, board, in Mr Tiffanys Long Island mansion with a small account for supplies. I cannot leave Dottie that long and besides this summer I want to come to California so I really do not know when I could accept it — but nevertheless I should appreciate the honor of the award.

Dottie told you of my designing job. I do not know what next then — but time will give we jobless people good fortune.

Fig. 2. "Aunt Flo" letter, c. 1928. Courtesy Dorothy Dehner

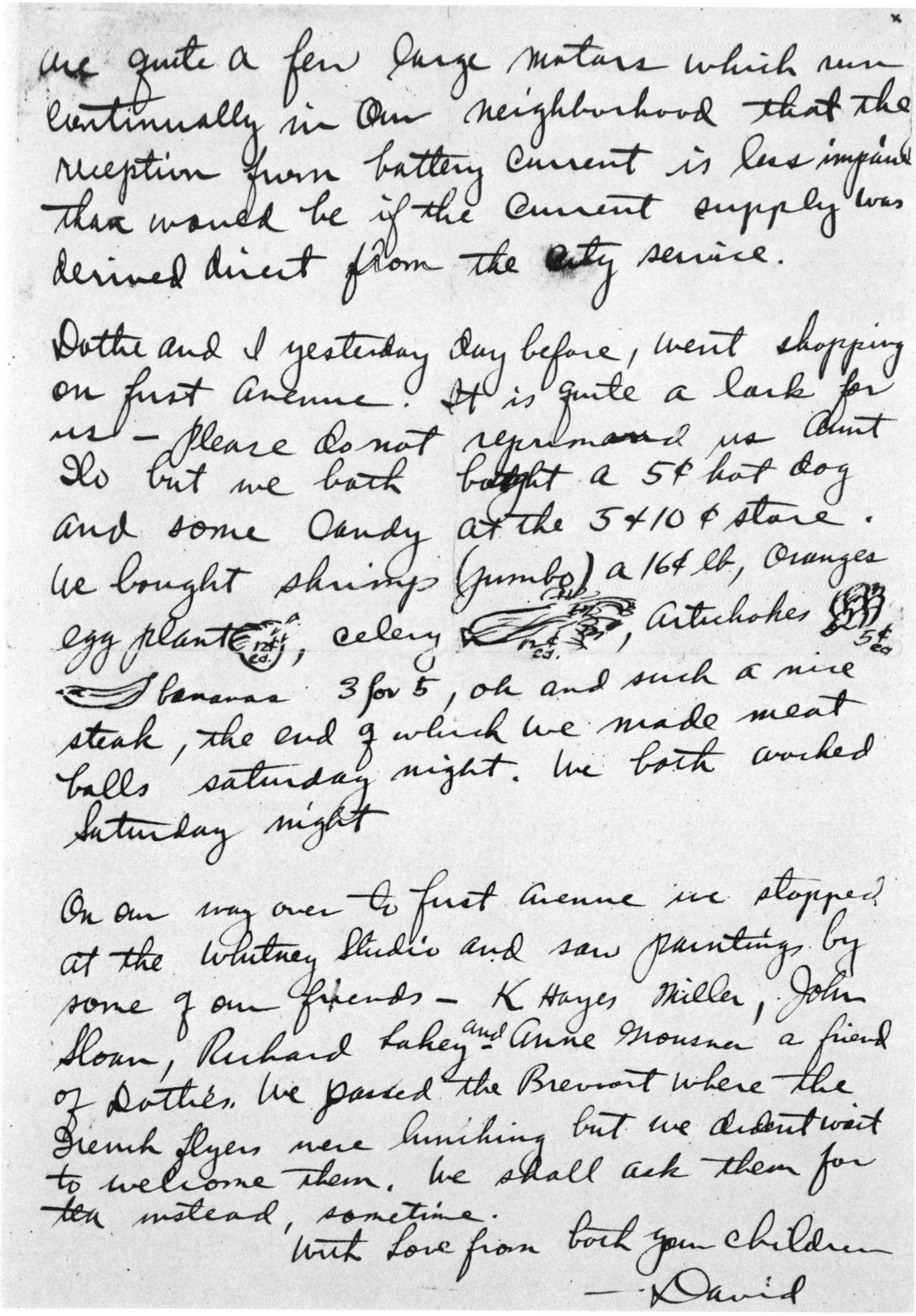

are quite a few large motors which run continually in our neighborhood that the reception from battery current is less impaired than would be if the current supply was derived direct from the city service.

Dottie and I yesterday day before, went shopping on first Avenue! It is quite a lark for us — Please do not reprimand us Aunt Flo but we both bought a 5¢ hot dog and some Candy at the 5 & 10¢ store. We bought shrimps (jumbo) a 16¢ lb, Oranges egg plant, celery, Artichokes 5¢ bananas 3 for 5, oh and such a nice steak, the end of which we made meat balls saturday night. We both worked Saturday night

On our way over to first Avenue we stopped at the Whitney Studio and saw paintings by some of our friends — K Hayes Miller, John Sloan, Richard Lahey and Anne Monsna a friend of Dottie's. We passed the Brevort where the French flyers were lunching but we didnt want to welcome them. We shall ask them for tea instead, sometime.

With love from both your children
— David

Fig. 3. ''Aunt Flo'' letter, c. 1928. Courtesy Dorothy Dehner

to see you both. I hope I will not disappoint you* but I do not feel like I'm making an acquaintance for I feel that I know you. When I knew about Dottie I knew about you and when ever with her I heard about you, and Sammie. Poor little Sammie he must have been an extraordinary dog. He probably has white wings and a little fuzzy white angel for his mate.

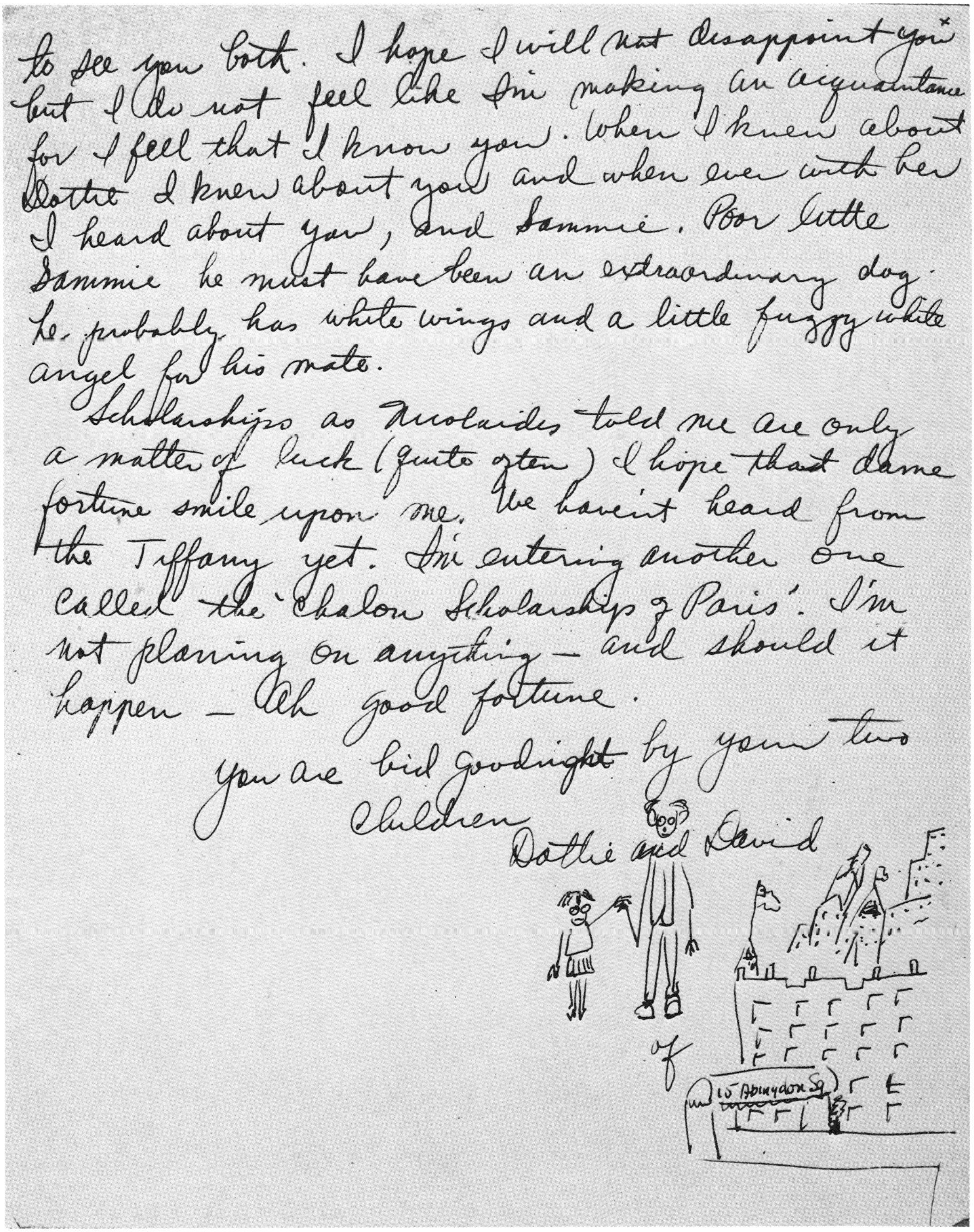

Scholarships as Nicolaides told me are only a matter of luck (quite often) I hope that dame fortune smile upon me. We haven't heard from the Tiffany yet. I'm entering another one called the "Chalon Scholarship of Paris". I'm not planing on anything — and should it happen — Oh good fortune.

You are bid goodnight by your two Children
Dottie and David

of

Fig. 4. "Aunt Flo" letter, c. 1928. Courtesy Dorothy Dehner

Fig. 5. David and Dorothy Smith, c. 1928. Courtesy Dorothy Dehner

find a place they could afford. What they found was Old Fox Farm, eighty-six acres with a small saltbox house on Tick Ridge Road. The house, which had been built in the 1820s, was unplanked and drafty. Water was pumped from a well that tended to run dry during the summer months. It was on this farm that the Terminal Iron Works, Smith's famous workshop, would eventually be located. The Smiths lived year-round in that house from 1940 to 1949, when a new house was finally completed.

Among their neighbors in Bolton Landing during the early 1930s were John and Elinor Graham and their son, David. John Graham was an important early influence on Smith, a source of encouragement and the person through whom Smith met the young Americans who were working in abstraction: Stuart Davis, Arshile Gorky, Milton Avery, Willem de Kooning, and Jean Xceron. (He later met Jackson Pollock on the Work Projects Administration.) At that time Graham painted in a severe nonobjective style. With Jan Matulka, he was responsible for Smith's early interest in Cubism. Until the end of his career, Smith continued to think of himself as a worker in that tradition. Graham's particular genius lay in his encouragement of struggling young artists. At a time when Smith did not yet consider himself to be primarily a sculptor, Graham was already calling him the best sculptor in America, just as he was calling de Kooning the best painter.[9]

Graham befriended young Smith in other ways. As the agent for Frank Crowninshield, then editor of *Vanity Fair,* Graham regularly traveled to Europe to purchase African art for the Crowninshield collection. Later he persuaded Crowninshield that Smith was the person to make the bases on which the African pieces were to sit. Smith received his first payment for making art. While in Paris, Graham attended discussion groups held in the studio of Joaquin Torres-Garcia and probably there met Julio Gonzalez, whose work he later introduced in the United States. Of even greater influence were the French art magazines that Graham brought back to the United States. The Smiths eagerly perused them in order to keep abreast of European art movements. It was an issue of *Cahiers d'art* which influenced Smith's decision to become a sculptor of welded steel.

As Graham's circle of young artists began to achieve success, Graham denigrated their importance as artists. Perhaps he was interested in struggling artists only so long as they continued to struggle. (Once a member of the tzarist cavalry and guard, Graham, born Ivan Dabrowsky, had joined the White Guard at the time of the Bolshevik Revolution.[10] Yet when he came to capitalist America, he espoused communism.) A strong advocate of Cubism when it was little understood or appreciated in this country, he rejected it as the movement gained wider acceptance. As the abstractionists developed Abstract Expressionism during the late 1940s, Graham broke with his disciples, including Smith.[11]

The year 1930 marked the first recorded public showing of a Smith work, a block print entitled *Interior Farm,* at the Print Club of Philadelphia. In that same year, Smith took a nighttime job as art editor of the magazine *Tennis.* Among his responsibilities were the magazine's layouts. (Since money was available for articles but not for layouts, the chief editor wrote stories under Smith's name in order to obtain funds for artwork.) While looking at a German magazine, *Gebrauchs-Graphik,* Smith came across the idea of "bleeding" a picture off the edge of the page, a technique not then in use in the United States. Smith began to apply the technique in his own layouts and eventually incorporated it in his art. In 1940 Marian Willard, then Smith's dealer, issued a press release on the *Medals for Dishonor* in which she specifically called attention to the way the elements broke out of the frame. After 1949, when Smith began to work with frontal sculptures whose flat surfaces were related to the picture planes of two-dimensional art, he consistently violated the plane with forms that protruded beyond it. In this way, Smith frequently stored away ideas that originated in other contexts, applying them many years later to his sculpture.

In September 1931 Smith left A. G. Spalding to travel with Dorothy by boat to Saint Thomas in the Virgin Islands. He remained there through May 1932, prowling the beaches to collect pebbles, broken shells, and fish bones. Smith continued to paint, but for the first time he also constructed several sculptures from bits of coral, wood, wire, pieces of lead,

Fig. 6. *Untitled,* c. 1933. Stone, lead, wire, on wood base. 2¼ × 3½ × 4⅛″. Collection Dorothy Dehner, New York. Photo by Stanley E. Marcus

30

and stones (c. 1933; Fig. 6). He also carved a coral head of a black, which he proceeded to paint a dark purplish brown. The trip to the Virgin Islands marked the end of art courses, the end of being an art student.

After his return from the Virgin Islands, Smith continued to incorporate bits and pieces of odd materials in his sculptures. The idea had probably originated in Matulka's class in 1928, where students had been encouraged to use all kinds of odd materials on their canvases. Of that class Smith wrote, "After my student period in painting . . . my paintings had turned to construct which had risen from the canvas so high that a base was required where the canvas should be. I now was a sculptor but there was no change in concept."[12] (It is interesting to note that of all the courses he had taken—at high school, by correspondence, at college and the Art Students' League—not one had to do with sculpture.)

Though still primarily a painter, Smith made sculptures in a small shed next to his Bolton Landing house. Skylights and windows were added to the shed, a forge and anvil were installed, and Smith now had his first workshop. His first metal connections were soldered. Later, during the summer of 1933, when Smith met the wife of the president of Union Carbide, he tried to persuade her to get him a welding outfit at wholesale. After trying and failing again in New York, he finally had to purchase a welding torch at retail.

In December 1932 the Smiths moved to Brooklyn Heights and David set to work on his welding in their living room. As the sparks flew, drawings on the walls and the curtains at the windows kept catching fire, and Dorothy rushed about with a watering can to douse the flames. On a walk one day along the Brooklyn waterfront, Dorothy noticed an old shed belonging to the Terminal Iron Works, where iron and steel were worked by a variety of methods. Smith rented a small area and moved in. When he had no money for rent, he would go out on jobs with the Terminal men, answer the phone, or, on a rare occasion, turn over a radio in payment. Smith often recalled with fondness the Brooklyn waterfront days and the companionship he enjoyed with the workers there. It was in that shed that Smith received his apprenticeship in the working of steel and mastered the art of welding, and it was that company's name that he eventually adopted for his own workshop.

Smith sold his first sculpture in 1933. John Graham brought Mrs. Lois Wright, a noted art patron, to the Smiths' Brooklyn Heights apartment, where a multimedia sculpture was displayed on a packing case in the living room. When Mrs. Wright offered to buy it, Smith was so delighted that he promptly presented her with a second piece.[13]

By September, a little over a year after he had produced his first sculpture, Smith wrote to Edgar Levy that "efforts are on sculpture and arrangements"[14] rather than oil painting, and that he had hopes that "Levy" (probably Julien Levy, one of the few New York dealers who were showing modern art at the time) would exhibit them. Smith's use of the word "arrangements" is significant. In differentiating among sculptures, oil paintings, and "arrangements," Smith was already visualizing a hybrid form that combined the two traditional media. This use of the term is our earliest clue to Smith's reluctance to be bound by orthodox categories and anticipates his later fusion of pictorial elements with sculptural techniques. Despite his statement that his efforts were concentrated on three-dimensional art, it should not be assumed that by 1933 Smith considered himself a sculptor. He would continue to vacillate between painting and sculpture until his return in 1936 from a trip to Europe.

In 1934 Smith went to work for the Temporary Emergency Relief Administration (TERA) as assistant project supervisor, an administrative nonrelief position. His job was to supervise the technical problems involved in the installation of murals in public buildings. Since, with his usual confidence, Smith had undertaken a position for which he had no training, he was compelled to cram by reading all the available material on the subject. But once his interest in the technical aspects of art had become aroused it never left him. From the time he began work with the TERA, Smith seemed far more interested in the way a work of art was put together than in the work itself. Notations in the sketchbooks made on his 1935–36 trip to Europe[15] continually refer to such concerns as the width of a crack in a Fra Angelico fresco, the quality of varnish on a Lucas Cranach painting, and the unjointing of the glued panels of fifteenth-century wood painting. The sketchbooks kept after the mid-1930s contain seemingly endless technical information on metals—their properties, techniques for their coloration, and methods of protecting them out-of-doors—and almost nothing about artists, either past or contemporary. It seems as though Smith was determined to wall himself off from the influence of other artists and to concern himself exclusively with observable phenomena. In this context, the significance of a well-known Smith statement becomes clear: "To me it is impossible to conceive two dimensions. I have seen a Chinese granite carving in the Boston museum and found its depth to be less than the thickness of paint in paintings by both Van Gogh and Cezanne."[16] Here is Smith the technical supervisor, ignoring style and content and limiting his observations to a work's physical properties, as he had earlier done in his sketchbook notations on his European trip. When the painter George Biddle wrote to the Public Buildings Administration in 1942 requesting information on the painting of murals, he found that both of the pamphlets he received had been written by Smith.[17] We must conclude that Smith felt himself more qualified to discuss the material of which art was composed than its aesthetics or content.

The early to mid-1930s was an awkward period in Smith's career. His student days were past but he was still neither painter nor sculptor. True, he had joined the ranks of young artists working on various federal art projects, but as a technician rather than as an artist. The number and variety of positions Smith held during those years reflect an unwillingness to commit himself. He did not need to earn his living. Dorothy's modest income was helpful in those Depression years, and Smith's small income from the TERA went primarily into materials and equipment for his art.

The sculptures he produced in the early 1930s did not seem promising. Using the human figure as a basis, Smith assembled various objects chosen for their resemblances to human features. Often he combined several materials and techniques, as in *Saw Head* of 1933 (Fig. 7). These very early works appear to be little more than crude welded versions of traditional monolithic forms.

In 1934, when Smith first showed his modest offerings, he began to attract the comments

Fig. 7. *Saw Head,* 1933. Iron. 18½ × 12 × 8¼″. Collection Candida and Rebecca Smith. Photo by David Smith

that would greatly heighten his sensitivity to criticism. Pierre Matisse is said to have informed Smith that his work looked better before it was unwrapped.[18] When the Smiths brought *Agricola Head* (1933; first known as *Man with Bandages*) into the Julien Levy Gallery, an artist who was then having a sculpture show there became furious and demanded its instant removal. Levy himself, though he showed two Smith works, was curious at first to know if the heads were held on with chewing gum and expressed concern that they might fall off.[19] Such remarks reflect the shock that must have been felt at those crude sculptures with their coarse surfaces. Yet the sculptures indicate a trait that Smith displayed from the very beginning of his career—an honesty of conviction. His rejection of the gleaming organic forms that characterized much of the sculpture of the 1930s reflects Smith's confidence in himself and his courage in acting on his beliefs. Even at a time when encouragement was of great importance and only a few artists supported him, Smith was unable to compromise.

3

EARLY USE
OF LINE

During an interview with the critic David Sylvester in 1961, Smith was asked what had inspired him to "turn from painting to sculpture suddenly."[1] His response, then and during other interviews, was that his interest had been caught by an illustration of an "iron sculpture" of Picasso's in either a 1928 or 1929 issue of *Cahiers d'art*. Two major myths about Smith arose from both the question and its answer: that Smith's transformation was sudden and that it had occurred sometime before 1930. A third, less serious misconception is that Picasso's 1929 *Construction in Wire* (see Fig. 8, 1972 enlarged version) had inspired the change; it did not appear in *Cahiers d'art* at that time. Picasso's 1928 *Project for a Sculpture in Iron Wire* (Fig. 9), a similar but substantially more anthropomorphic piece, did appear in the 1929 issue of *Cahiers d'art*, and undoubtedly was the one that Smith saw.[2]

It was not until 1936 that Smith concentrated on sculpture. Smith's first sculptures were not made until 1932, in the Virgin Islands, several years after he claimed to have seen Picasso's *Project*. Over the next several years Smith continued to paint as well as to construct his "arrangements." A frequently repeated story—verified by Dorothy Dehner, who was present at the time—is that John Graham and John Xceron exhorted Smith in 1935 to concentrate on sculpture.[3] There would have been no need for them to do so if Smith had already abandoned painting for sculpture. The strongest evidence, however, that in 1935 Smith was still putting his main effort into painting is found in letters written from Europe by David and Dorothy to the Edgar Levys. (The Smiths sailed for France in the fall of 1935. Most of the money for the trip came from a helpful exchange of bonds between Dorothy and her aunt Florence Uphof. A small amount came from Smith's parents. Before they finally returned home, nearly a year later, they had visited Greece, Russia, and England.) The letters to the Levys indicate that Smith was having considerable difficulty with his painting, though the nature of that difficulty is not disclosed. At one point Smith seems to have grown a bit more optimistic; he wrote that his work had improved and his painting was "getting level."[4] Whatever that meant, it did not last. Later Dorothy wrote that Smith had become sick of Greece and had committed several acts of violence in frustration over his lack of progress.[5] During his later interview with David Sylvester, Smith reflected that his European trip confirmed his belief that he worked best in the United

Fig. 8. Pablo Picasso. *Monument,* 1972. (Constructed after an enlargement, supervised by the artist, of a 20″ wire maquette from 1928–29 of a monument to Guillaume Apollinaire.) Steel. 155⅝″ high, including base 1⅞ × 58¾ × 125¾″. Collection and photo courtesy The Museum of Modern Art, New York. Gift of the artist. Photo by John Webb

36

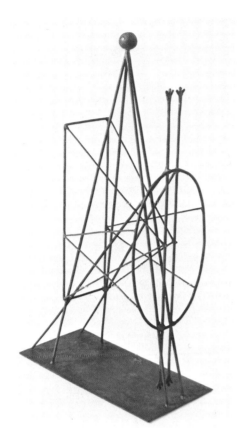

Fig. 9. Pablo Picasso. *Construction (Project for a Sculpture in Iron Wire),* 1928–29. Steel. 150 × 39 × 77". Collection Musée Picasso, Paris. Photo © SPADEM, Paris/ VAGA, New York, 1982

States. He could have added that the trip also convinced him to change from his emphasis on painting, though he would continue to paint until the end of his life.

In a well-known and often repeated statement, Smith said, "I do not recognize the limits where painting ends and sculpture begins. . . . there is a difference in degree in actual space and the absolute difference in gravity."[6] Strangely, for someone who began his career as a painter, Smith repeatedly referred to paint as "mass" and ignored it as color. Herman Cherry, a painter who became a close friend, noted that Smith had little color sense. Perhaps this observation offers a clue to the nature of Smith's painting difficulties in Europe. By conceiving of painting and sculpture as materials occupying space, Smith could ignore the differences between the two.

Though the letters from Europe indicate that Smith was concentrating on painting, the die was finally cast in favor of sculpture sometime during that same period. Either just before they left for Europe or soon after their return, Dorothy wrote the Levys that Smith had moved his small shed in Bolton Landing away from the barn (presumably to avoid setting it on fire) so that he could use it for welding. "He is so keen about it that the stonewall is for the nonce neglected."[7] What had aroused Smith's enthusiasm was the publication of several photographs of Gonzalez's sculptures in *Cahiers d'art* (Fig. 10). She

Fig. 10. Julio Gonzalez. Untitled sculpture, c. 1934–35. Illustrated in *Cahiers d'art,* 1935. Reproduced by permission of Carmen Martinez

38

and David, she said, had become greatly excited by the way the forms went "swinging off into space and . . . Smith wished he could do the same."[8] It was his attempts to do so in 1936 that first carried Smith's work well away· from the early amalgams of objects assembled in roughly the form of the human figure and into the first truly creative art of his career. The prominent use of rods in the 1936 works indicates that Smith remembered Picasso's *Project for a Sculpture* and was ready at last to put that technique to use.

Early in his career, the patterns made by line had fascinated Smith. This interest may well have been fostered by his work for the TERA, an important responsibility of which was to advise muralists on ways of preventing cracks in walls from reappearing in their murals. Line seemed a mystical force to Smith, particularly in drawing. Smith had planned to use rods to create lines on a flat surface. "The line contour with its variations and its comment on mass space is more acute than bulk shape. In vision the overlay of shapes seen through each other not only permits each shape to retain its individual intent but in juxtaposition highly multiplies the association of the new and more complex unity."[9] Unfortunately, when lines overlie each other, the result does not necessarily "highly multiply the associations," but can diminish them, since the wire's bulk intrudes. The consequence is often confusion instead of new images. It is for this reason that wire images, to be clearly recognizable, are usually silhouetted. This is probably the reason that in his 1950 and 1951 "drawings in air," a series of linear works, Smith was compelled to use a flat format. In comparison with line drawings, the flattened wire works are necessarily simplistic. Smith must have recognized that he could not generate sufficient imagery through the use of wire to sustain a large body of work. By 1951 the spatial-drawing period was over. Smith never returned to use of wire.

As the 1930s advanced, the importance of image making in Smith's work grew and the limitations of wire in this respect became apparent. Three works, *Aerial Construction* (1936; Fig. 11), *Interior,* and *Interior for Exterior,* exemplify the changing relationship between Smith's use of line and his subject matter. *Aerial Construction* shows Smith's emphasis on line and only minimal interest in subject. He used the classic Cubist device of the guitar as a point of departure. At the right, the strings and sounding hole are in recognizable order, as if the guitar has been laid on its side. But as we scan the composition from right to left, it breaks down: where we expect to find the sounding board, we see instead a random pattern of planes, real and implied, weaving back and forth in shallow depth. This entire section is alive with activity. The interplay of real planes—small pieces of sheet metal—and implied ones is essential to any wire construction in depth in order to avoid the kind of chaos that exists in *Star Cage* (1950; Fig. 12). In *Aerial Construction,* Smith avoided a breakdown of order by making several of the planes explicit, a device he had first employed in 1935 in *Reclining Figure* and which was more noticeable in *Suspended Figure* of the same year.

The inconsistency of *Aerial Construction,* with its almost representational right side and its nonobjective left, reflects the dilemma facing many artists who have not yet developed a mature style. Even those who see themselves as nonobjective artists usually at some stage in their development work from nature. In April 1948 Smith wrote Edgar Levy, "Only

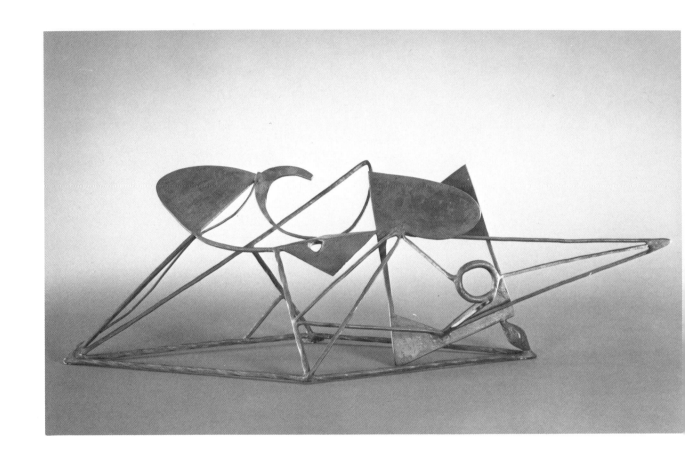

Fig. 11. *Aerial Construction,* 1936. Painted and welded iron. 10 × 30⅞ × 11½″. Collection and photo courtesy Hirshhorn Museum and Sculpture Garden, Smithsonian Institution, Washington, D.C.

Fig. 12. *Star Cage,* 1950. Steel. 44¾ × 52¼ × 28″. Collection University Gallery, University of Minnesota, Minneapolis, John Rood Sculpture Collection. Photo by David Smith

occasionally can I start out with no preconceived subject or point. I usually have a drawing for the start.''[10] Because all of *Aerial Construction*'s recognizable elements are located on the right, it is logical to suppose that this part of the work was constructed first. We can speculate that after starting with the idea of a guitar, Smith fashioned the neck, strings, and hole before moving onto the sounding board, which he then broke up into facets. Both the use of a frontal orientation instead of rounded monolithic form and the immediacy of welding technique make it possible to scan or read this work from right to left. Had Smith not been working directly with his material but, for example, in wax, as for bronze casting, he could have reworked his forms so that the inconsistency among successive elements would have been eliminated.

By 1937 Smith had become more concerned with the subject than with its form. No doubt the rapid sweep of interest in Surrealism in the United States influenced him. In Paris, during his 1935 European tour, Smith had already seen a Surrealist exhibition and visited Paul Eluard's house to see Meret Oppenheim's *Fur-lined Teacup*.[11] The Museum of Modern Art's ''Fantastic Art, Dada, Surrealism'' exhibition of December 1936 to January 1937 drew a large attendance. Julien Levy held annual Surrealist exhibitions, and even department-store windows had surrealistic themes. It is not surprising that Smith, still very much in the formative stages of his development, was influenced by all this excitement. He was not, however, looking to break down his psychic defenses to reach the subconscious, as were the Surrealists. Instead there was a deliberate probing of symbols, particularly sexual ones. The sketchbooks of the 1930s and forties are full of examples that bare evidence of careful, repetitious reworking over a span of months and even years. In one sketchbook Smith wrote of ''recurrences of totemism the subjects and directions dictated by totems and the sense of guilt''[12] as being the basis of modern aesthetics. As we will see later, the conscious repetition and manipulation of the bird-head totems eventually contributed heavily to the development of modular forms.

Smith's turn to figurative and quasi-figurative art, which preoccupied him until 1950, can be seen in *Interior* (1937; Fig. 13), though that work still retains some abstraction. For his theme Smith chose an artist's studio. In both his choice of subject, a tradition of nineteenth-century painting, and its frontal orientation, Smith revealed his continued interest in painting.

Interior demonstrates Smith's struggle to reconcile line and subject. We may presume that the left side of the work was constructed first, since it is more representational than the rest and more closely linked with the original point of departure, an artist's studio. One of the two tables on the left holds a modeled female figure; the other holds three rounded forms related to the ball-and-wire motif of the sculpture. That motif had its origins in Picasso's thematic use of dot and line. Smith used it frequently during the 1930s and occasionally thereafter throughout his career.

The style of the middle section is altogether different, a confusion of seemingly random lines interweaving in shallow space. The tall triangle on the left with a ball perched atop it represents the roofline of the structure, a reading supported by similar imagery in two other works. *Interior for Exterior* also contains a circular form atop its roofline. In a third

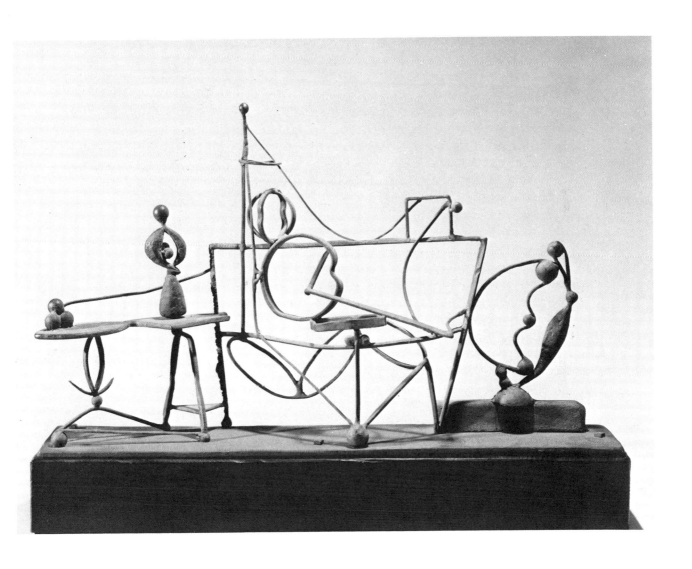

Fig. 13. *Interior,* 1937. Steel and bronze. 15¼ × 26 × 5¼″ on wood base. Collection Weatherspoon Art Gallery, University of North Carolina at Greensboro.

43

Fig. 14. *Home of the Welder*, 1945. Steel. 21 × 17¾ × 13⅝″. Collection Candida and Rebecca Smith. Photo courtesy Knoedler Contemporary Art

Fig. 15. *Home of the Welder,* back view. Photo courtesy Knoedler Contemporary Art

45

interior, *Home of the Welder* (1945; Figs. 14, 15), the curved form perches on top of the room and from it emerge lines that twist and stretch. The roofline has been removed to the far end of the room, and the mast, here separated from the roofline, bears a striking resemblance to that of *Interior*.

As we continue to scan *Interior* from left to right, our eyes are led to the rather strangely formed third segment. Smith may have intended this form to represent the artist, but since it is so isolated from the modeled form on the table, he may have had another purpose. Visually it seems to have been intended as a counterweight to the forms on the left and to contain the sprawl of the linear middle. In effect, the work has an *a-b-a* composition.

When we compare *Interior* with the earlier *Aerial Construction*, it is evident that Smith was turning from abstraction to more active involvement with his subject. *Aerial Construction* used its guitar subject as a prop for the real one, an interweaving of real and implied planes through space. By contrast, *Interior's* scene is based on life; the ball-and-wire motif is of only secondary importance.

In *Interior for Exterior* (1939; Fig. 16), the importance of wire as an aesthetic component was substantially reduced. Though there is still expression in the way lines are formed and in other elements as well, the essence of this work lies in meanings beyond what is seen. In this work Smith had begun to create a much more personal art. *Interior for Exterior* is less dependent on borrowed themes, whether from art history (the artist's studio, reclining figures) or from contemporary artists (Picasso's dot and line) than had been the case in Smith's earlier work. Still the work is derivative, in this instance almost surely based on Alberto Giacometti's *Palace at 4 A.M.* (1932–33; Fig. 17).[13] Both are wire dwellings and as such allow what is within their walls to be visible. Inside of each there are mysterious forms that because of their juxtaposition appear to interact. Both the Giacometti and the Smith have snakelife forms rising from the floor. In the Giacometti a prehistoric bird attempts to soar from its cage, while in the Smith it is a female figure with outstretched arms who actually breaks from the confining frame.

For all their similarities, however, the differences are more important: in those differences lie Smith's efforts to become his own man. The Giacometti images are precise. Each form is fully developed; its purpose may not be clear but there is no question as to its contours. On the other hand, Smith's forms are more obscure, as though he still did not feel ready to commit himself to a particular image. Forms flow into one another, blurring boundaries. Smith's sketchbooks from the late 1930s to the mid-1940s bear witness to what must have been arduous working-over of ideas before a settling on particular symbols to represent them. In many instances, the resulting forms were then incorporated into sculptures. By the mid-1940s, Smith had developed a vocabulary of specific images. As the forms became more clear in his mind, through his sketches, they assumed precise contours in the sculptures. *Interior for Exterior* seems to have been the catalyst for his taking that direction: the giant key in the door seems symbolic, as if Smith knew this work was going to open new vistas. As he developed more clearly defined images, Smith stopped using rods and with it abandoned the expressive qualities that characterized his work of the mid-1930s. The rod lines of *Interior for Exterior* were more than mere supports and frames

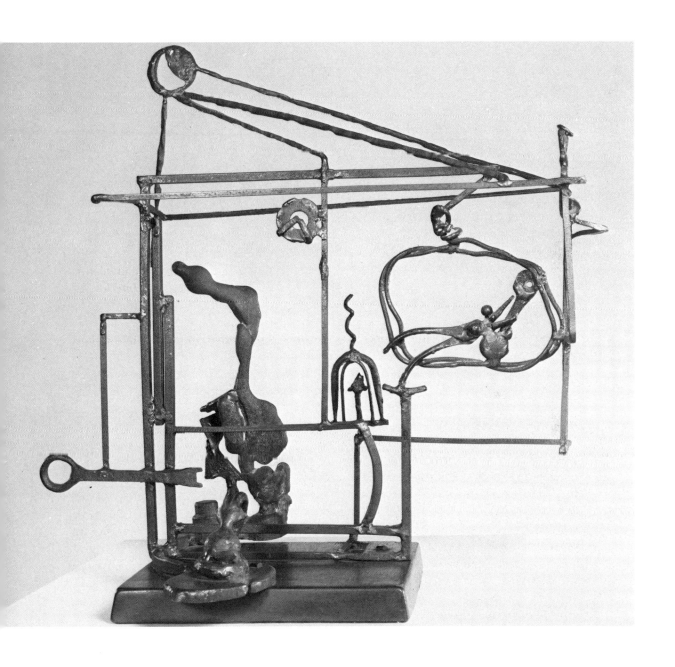

Fig. 16. *Interior for Exterior,* 1939. Steel and bronze. 18 × 22 × 23¼″. Private collection. Photo by Jonas Portrait Photography, Pittsburgh

Fig. 17. Alberto Giacometti. *The Palace at 4 A.M.,* 1932–33. Wood, glass, wire, string. 25 × 28¼ × 15¾″. Collection and photo courtesy The Museum of Modern Art, New York. Purchase

(as was the case in Giacometti's *Palace at 4 A.M.*): they possessed, in addition, an inherent expressive quality. The abandonment of rods was accompanied by a loss of lyricalness.

The developing symbolism reached its peak in *Home of the Welder*, a piece for which *Interior for Exterior* had been the model. So strong was the imagery of *Home of the Welder* that Edward Fry described it as "one of the greatest examples of autopsychoanalysis in the history of modern art."[14] Wire was inadequate to carry the heavy load of symbolism and literary reference that Smith now put into his work. He turned completely to solid forms, as he had turned from the wire walls of *Interior for Exterior* to the solid ones of *Home of the Welder*. The ambiguities created by rods, witnessed even in the title "Interior for Exterior," had to be resolved through the use of solid forms if specific images were to be developed; but the welding process by itself proved insufficient. Smith began to use casting, brazing, silver soldering, and jewelry tools to develop specific forms.

Smith did not return to a basically welded format until 1950. When he did, wire was once again his material, just as in the mid-1930s he had used it for expressive purposes. Those lyrical lines of the sculptures of the fifties were destined to link Smith with the New York Group of painters and were in fact termed "drawings in air."[15]

4

FROM ABSTRACTION
TO SYMBOLISM

In 1937, after his return from Europe, Smith went to work for the Treasury Department, conducting a survey of post offices in preparation for a government mural project. Eventually he became an artist for the Work Projects Administration, and produced several sculptures under its auspices before he finally left in 1939.

The late 1930s was a difficult period for abstract artists. The first American Artists' Congress met in New York's Town Hall in February 1936. Illustrations in the catalogue for its second exhibition show only statuary and busts. Of that period Smith wrote, "One just kept working and nothing publicly happened. . . . The authorities all declaimed and in unity declared the abstract concept dead. . . . Presumably, so were we."[1] He had learned the value of publicity during his stint as a promoter of sports equipment for A. G. Spalding, however, and he was not about to be ignored. He stirred up his first controversy in 1938, at an Artists' Congress exhibition. All entries were placed on pedestals that had been painted pink. Smith raised strong objections to the color; he insisted on a neutral white for his own pedestals. The Exhibition Committee rejected his complaint as trivial: all pedestals were properly painted the same color. (It is interesting that several years later when Marian Willard painted Smith's *Ad Mare* battleship gray for an exhibition at the Metropolitan Museum of Art, Smith did not complain.)[2]

Gradually Smith became known. In early 1937 the Boyer Gallery in New York showed *Suspended Figure, Construction,* and *Figure Construction.* In the same year Hananiah Harari saw Smith's work being photographed at Leo Lance's studio and recommended it to the young art dealer Marian Willard.[3] Willard went to Brooklyn Heights to see Smith's work and was impressed. She offered him the opportunity to take part in a group show at her East River Gallery, but Smith insisted on a one-man exhibition. Willard agreed, and seventeen of Smith's works, executed from 1935 through 1937, were shown at the beginning of 1938.

The importance of Marian Willard to the development of Smith's career has never been properly recognized. A woman whose interest in art grew out of a background of wealth and refinement, she has a quality of reserve not usually associated with the competitive art world. Her eye for talent is superb. On a trip to Switzerland in 1937 she bought the work of Paul Klee and arranged to show it in the United States—one of the first American dealers to do so; she also handles the work of Mark Tobey and Morris Graves. There is little likelihood that Marian Willard's account books show anything but losses on Smith during the eighteen years that she represented him. As late as 1950, when Smith was being acknowledged by some critics as the most important sculptor in America, he could still show only three hundred dollars in sales. Nevertheless, scarcely a year went by that Marian Willard did not give Smith a one-man show. Smith's output grew prodigiously, and the gallery as well as her home in Locust Valley, New York, overflowed with his works. She continually brought his work to the attention of collectors, critics, and museums. She cultivated writers and sent publicity releases or personal letters to anyone who could help Smith's career. She sent him leads on lectures and jobs. In times of hardship, she advanced him money or bought a small work from him. When Smith did not have enough money to pay his share of the costs of an exhibition, he photographed and installed the works himself, and Willard accepted a small piece at its list price. There was no romantic attachment between them; Willard's only motivation seems to have been an unshakable conviction that Smith was destined to be recognized as a major artist.

The image Smith created for himself during the late 1930s, that of steelworker turned artist, had an inherent danger. While the novelty of the image attracted considerable publicity, it was publicity of the wrong kind. In an article entitled "Sewer Pipe Sculpture," which appeared in *Cue* magazine on March 16, 1940, the author wondered if Smith could shoe horses or catch rivets in a bucket. An article in *Popular Science* of July 1940, entitled "Blacksmith-Sculptor Forges Art," discussed steelworking techniques. Ernest Watson's "From Studio to Forge," published in *American Artist* in March 1940, did make a sincere attempt to picture Smith as a serious artist. Even so, fascination with the novelty remained ("The imagination falters at the prospect of cutting a nude from steel plate a half-inch or more thick"), and once again Smith was dealt with as a craftsman rather than as an artist. Smith received his most scathing criticism, however, in the April 22, 1940, issue of *Time* magazine. The article "Screwball Art" likened Smith's work to "plumbing that has survived a conflagration." (Smith was not alone, though: the author also described Surrealists as artists who try to put nightmares and nervous breakdowns on canvas.)

Not all critics let the novelty of Smith's work blind them to its art. Elizabeth McCausland, writing about *Medals for Dishonor* for the *Springfield* (Massachusetts) *Republican* in November 1940, thoroughly described Smith's technique and yet dealt with his artistic beliefs with great sensitivity. Her efforts may well have helped Smith to clarify his own thoughts. After Smith's first exhibition, Carlyle Burrows, of the *New York Herald Tribune*, described Smith as a virtually unknown artist but one who promised to be much discussed. A less optimistic Jerome Klein of the *New York Post* believed Smith to be ponderously following Picasso and Pablo Gargallo in making twisted, abstract sequences. Smith's metal "carcasses," he wrote, had no "heart." Howard Devree of the *New York Times* cautiously appraised Smith's works as complicated mechanical constructions that seemed to await the hand of Alexander Calder to set them in motion—earnest endeavors in a heavily modern, decorative style. The *Daily Worker,* reviewing the American Abstract Artists' Exhibit at the National Academy in December 1937—perhaps taking literally the legend of Smith the workingman—called Smith's work the most original in the show and rich in contemporary associations.

In those years Smith was vacillating between pure art and craft. For a time he even considered going into business as a craftsman. His interest in craftwork began in early 1939, when John McAndrews, of the Museum of Modern Art, asked him if he would consider a commission to fashion andirons, tongs, and a shovel for the museum's Members' Room. Smith did the work. A few months later a similar request came from the Metropolitan Museum of Art for a display of industrial art. In a 1940 interview by Maude Riley in *Cue* magazine, Smith expanded his factory career at Studebaker to a year and a half and said that if his "market" didn't materialize soon, he would make andirons by the dozen for department stores. In late 1941, picking up the idea he had pursued in *Medals for Dishonor*, Smith began to make "medallion pins," which he hoped to sell commercially as jewelry. In early 1942, Marian Willard had to tell Smith that he was not known for making pins. In August 1942 a dismayed Smith acknowledged his mistake in thinking that the pin investment "was going to be quick return."[4]

Though such commercial ventures proved unsuccessful for Smith, the public displayed an interest in the use of industrial tools to make art, and Smith was not adverse to taking advantage of it. The publicity was seductive. The novelty of his way of making art and the craftsmanship with which it was made created an interested audience. Yet the result was wrong. Smith was using his welding torch as an alternative means of reproducing traditional ideas that were based on totally different techniques and materials. The result would never be more than a poor substitute. If Smith was to avoid being derivative, he must exploit the inherent capabilities of his material and techniques. But such reasoning ran counter to the accepted belief, to which Smith also ascribed, that art based on technique and material was necessarily craft-oriented and thus of lesser stature than fine art. Smith never reconciled himself to the fact that it was his welding technique that ultimately determined the nature of his art.

In June 1938 Marian Willard suggested to Wallace Harrison, the architect and designer of the Trylon and Perisphere symbols for the upcoming New York World's Fair (1939–40) that Smith make a forged metal sculpture for one of the buildings. There is no record of Smith obtaining a commission. In the same year he was asked to serve as an alternate on the committee that chose sculptures to be shown at the Fair. The widespread excitement over the Fair evidently was the catalyst that promoted Smith's interest in the relationship of sculpture to architecture. Since he had previously worked in the Treasury Department's division of painting and sculpture, he was familiar with the requirement that a small percentage of the cost of each new government building be allocated to its adornment, often sculptural. With the advent of the Fair and its use of modernistic buildings, Smith began to see buildings as sculptures: "Outside of NYC and a few larger cities sculpture can take on structure, proportions and it can tower above buildings. It can have a view from distance, from moving vehicles on ground and transport by air . . . the vision of mountains, forests, air beacons at night, moving or static arouse an aesthetic stimuli. Two geometric forms such as cone and sphere are appreciated."[5] The sketchbooks of 1939 indicate Smith's obsession with the Trylon and Perisphere, as he worked and reworked the Fair's symbols into abstract and symbolic drawings. In a then-unpublished article, "Modern Sculpture and Society," written about 1940, Smith described the need for a new way to perceive sculpture; that is, according to architectural principles.[6]

In that same article are found the beginnings of Smith's assault on monolithic sculpture. He wrote that the public generally accepted open lines and space in architecture, and then he proceeded to criticize the "bourgeoisie" (although he never makes clear who they are) for failing to accept the same principles in modern sculpture. In her *Terminal Iron Works*, Rosalind Krauss wrote of the vogue for stone carving during the 1930s and referred to the tendency to call such an art "progressive." Krauss pointed out that much of Smith's antagonism to monolithic sculpture was born of the tight grip that stone carving held on sculptural art in the thirties and his need to challenge it.[7] As Smith said in 1951: "My concept as an artist is a revolt against the well-worn beauties in the form of a statue. Rather I would prefer my assemblages to be the savage idols of basic patterns."[8]

The Fair's role in Smith's developing "savage idols" is revealed in *Blue Construction* (1938), which was exhibited there. Doris Brian wrote in *Art News* that the work's strong linear forces made it the Fair's most distinguished abstraction. For several years before 1939, Smith had been using Picasso's dot-and-line motif. In *Blue Construction, Head* (1938; see Fig. 24), and *Ad Mare* (1939) among others, the balls and wires were turned into the spherical and pyramidal shapes of the Trylon and Perisphere. Smith made a second modification of the sphere/pyramid motif by eliminating the sphere and elongating the pyramid into a threatening, clawlike form. The sketchbooks that Smith kept during the late 1930s and early 1940s blatantly reveal the metamorphosis of the Fair's symbols into sexual symbols. As *Egyptian Landscape* (1951; Fig. 18) so graphically illustrates, with its pyramids joined at the bottom to form the shape of female genitalia and the sphere with a metal bar appended to form a phallus shape, Smith continued to use the sphere-and-pyramid motif as a sexual symbol for many years.

Smith rarely, if ever, acknowledged the sources that influenced his work. Throughout his career he seemed to cast himself in the role of a loner struggling to escape the dominance of powerful forces. Emily Genauer, who wrote with great sympathy about Smith's efforts, saw his 1938 exhibition and nearly twenty years later remembered him as an angry young man who was seething with bitterness about the state of the world.[9] The 1938–40 *Medals for Dishonor* constituted the opening shot in a war against institutions, which continued during the 1940s as Smith vented his personal grievances in the guise of moral indignation. By embellishing his working-class experiences he cast himself as an intruder in the lush sanctums of midtown Manhattan galleries. By moving permanently to the isolation of Bolton Landing in 1940, he was rejecting the New York art world that had rejected his work. He was also publicly dissociating himself from the influences and values of that world. He would not admit to being indebted to any artist or school, except in the vaguest terms.

In the late 1930s Smith had not yet broken away from several early influences. Perhaps the most important work of that period, *Structure of Arches* (1939; Fig. 19), contains

Fig. 18. *Egyptian Landscape,* 1951. Steel painted with red primer and bronze. 26¾ × 49⅝ × 18¾″. Private collection. Photo by David Smith

Fig. 19. *Structure of Arches,* 1939. Steel. 39 × 48 × 30″. Collection Addison Gallery of American Art, Phillips Academy, Andover, Mass. Gift of Mrs. R. Crosby Kemper. Photo by Smith Studio, Glens Falls, New York

evidence of two of those influences, the World's Fair and the sculpture of Alberto Giacometti. Elongated pyramids dominate the work, and in the circle atop one of them we see lingering evidence of the spheres he had used earlier. This work, however, is not devoted simply to variations on the sphere-and-pyramid theme, but transcends its motif to achieve an architectural quality. That quality stems from the way the elongated pyramids loom over ground-hugging elements. Smith succeeded in capturing abstractly the atmosphere of the World's Fair itself with its massive, geometrical buildings surrounded by low-lying walkways.

The influence of Giacometti's work of the early 1930s is also apparent in *Structure of Arches*. As mentioned earlier, the Smiths had access to *Cahiers d'art* through John Graham. We can assume that Smith saw the 1932 issue that contained a photograph of Giacometti's *Femme angoissée dans une chambre la nuit* (Anguished Woman in a Room at Night, 1932), a work quite similar in form to his *Femme égorgée* (Woman with Her Throat Cut, 1932; Fig. 20), which Smith probably had also seen. Both of these works, which are intended to be placed on the floor, convey a strong sense of male dominance over supine and helpless women. Smith assimilated this idea and used it in *Structure of Arches*. The relationship is not apparent until one recognizes that the two small pyramidal forms on the bottom bar are symbolic breasts, a device Smith frequently used during the forties and fifties. In Giacometti's works we see only the females; the males have done their violence and gone. Smith supplied the masculine forms, sharply pointed pyramids that loom over less angular female forms. The difference in point of view characterizes the difference between Smith's and Giacometti's views of their art. Giacometti, here and in his later cityscapes, strove for greater visibility of his forms by presenting an unobstructed view from above. Smith's works force us into continual movement around them as we attempt to see their forms—yet no matter what position we take, the perspective remains blocked by some of the elements; we are not really permitted to grasp the full nature of his work. With the developing sexual symbolism that emerges in this work and with the introduction of clawlike forms, Smith entered a period of demonology which, because of the demands of the techniques involved, would lead him far from the exploitation of welding as an art form. "Form will flower with spikes of steel.[10]

The *Medals for Dishonor* (1938–40; Fig. 21) brought Smith his first real attention as a serious artist. The anger manifest in that series of images became focal in Smith's work during the next ten years, as abstraction was all but forgotten. So consistent is the theme of anger throughout that some of the works of the 1940s seem to have an almost therapeutic dimension, as if Smith were working out his inner tensions. Yet these sculptures have an attraction beyond the excellence of their craftmanship and became the basis of Smith's early reputation. In these sculptures obvious symbols are combined with strange, sinister forms. *Home of the Welder*, which Fry so extravagantly praised for its autobiographical significance, comments on marriage with a massive millstone through which dangles an equally conspicuous chain of steel, both prominently placed to leave no doubt as to their meaning. The "Spectre" series of the mid-1940s is directly related to the *Medals for Dishonor* through its images of additional targets for Smith's anger. One of the series, *Race*

Fig. 20. Alberto Giacometti. *Woman with Her Throat Cut,* 1932. Bronze (cast 1949). 8 × 34½ × 25″. Collection and photo courtesy The Museum of Modern Art, New York. Purchase

Fig. 21. *Medals for Dishonor: War Exempt Sons of the Rich,* 1938–40. Bronze. 10¼ × 9⅛ × ⅞″. Collection Hirshhorn Museum and Sculpture Garden, Smithsonian Institution, Washington, D.C. Photo by O. E. Nelson, courtesy Marlborough Gallery, New York

for Survival (1946), Smith called a picture of hate.[11] *Spectre of Mother* (1946; Fig. 22) depicts a woman blowing a long tulip-shaped form (women blowing trumpets was one of Smith's graphic themes) while she dangles a child upside down. In *Pillar of Sunday* (1945) Smith lashed out at the Church and those who support it. His last such angry attack, *The Sacrifice* (1950), was also directed at the Church.

As Smith moved in this new direction, he became increasingly determined to clarify his images. To do so he needed a precision not attainable with the welding torch. He experimented with a variety of methods, including dentists' and jewelers' techniques, as well as the traditional method of sculpture, casting. With no training in any of these techniques, Smith set out on a course similar to the one he took in teaching himself about mural painting for the TERA in 1934. Smith filled his sketchbooks during 1939 and 1940 with a hodgepodge of notes as he laboriously acquired the knowledge necessary for executing *Medals for Dishonor*. Though a professional jewelry foundry did the actual casting—Smith himself did not make a successful casting until 1949—he had to learn all of the preparatory steps to the process as well as the cleanup and patination. Elizabeth McCausland, in the *Springfield* (Massachusetts) *Sunday Union and Republican* of November 10, 1940, gives considerable insight into the patience, skill, and knowledge Smith had to acquire to make the *Medals* and reveals much about the processes he had to employ to achieve control over his forms. It is not surprising that as Smith mastered this complex of skills he took considerable pride in his accomplishments—and therein lay the trap. His accomplishments were those of the master craftsman, and they diverted him far from the path he had once followed as an artist creating art with a welding torch.

Smith began the *Medals* with notes and sketches. Some of the images were not preceded by formal drawings, but for others he traced drawings directly on plaster blanks. Then began the difficult task of learning to see in reverse. Instead of carving out an object, as an artist ordinarily would do to make a sculpture in stone, Smith had to make a negative mold: he had to carve from the plaster the space that would eventually be filled by the final material, either bronze or silver. Time and again he had to "prove" the negative by pressing plasticene into it so that the positive form could be seen. For a year or more Smith painstakingly worked at reverse carving, frequently shattering the plaster casts with his clumsy tools until, at the suggestion of his dentist, he switched to dental tools. After completing the negative, he cast a positive form into the mold with plastic dental stone, which is harder than the plaster of the mold. Using a sensitive separator to avoid chemical disintegration of the plaster, Smith then removed the casting from its mold. As he did so, the harder casting ripped away unnoticed undercuts in the mold, those pieces of the mold that would have locked in the casting and prevented it from being pulled clear. The elimination of undercuts was important, as Smith intended to strike his medals on dies. The dental stone permitted him to see the corrections needed on the positive before he made his master bronze.

The original plan, to stamp out medals on dies, would have produced strikes of clear, sharp lines. Smith had acquired a knowledge of dies at the Studebaker factory, where they had been used on the assembly line to stamp out fenders and oil pans. Smith saw the

Fig. 22. *Spectre of Mother,* 1946. Steel and stainless steel. 20⅜ × 23⅝ × 9¼″ on wood base. Collection Sidney Feldman, Bal Harbor, Florida. Photo by Robert E. Mates, courtesy David McKee Gallery, New York

possibility of editions in the hundreds, even thousands. The cost of dies was prohibitive, however, so Smith decided instead to produce one of each image by casting. Since the quantity was too small to interest a commercial foundry, he turned to one that cast pieces of jewelry. In his own first attempts at casting, in 1936 and 1937, he had poured tin into iron negatives. The foundry to which he now went used a mixture of tin, lead, and zinc with bronze. The master bronze was tamped down in a core box of sand and then removed, leaving a negative impression in the sand. After the sand mold was delicately dusted, to prevent the metal from later sticking to the sand, it was baked. Metal was poured while the mold was still hot in order to secure sharp detail. Smith did his own buffing, chasing, and oxidizing. The "medals" were then fixed to wooden plaques. Of the fifteen *Medals*, only one, the third, was cast in silver; the rest were of bronze.

The *Medals* not only anticipated the monolithic, demonic symbolic works of the 1940s, but, as a kind of drawing, anticipated the "drawings in air" sculptures of the 1950s. Smith's vacillation between two-dimensional and three-dimensional art continued. In a letter of February 6, 1941,[12] Marian Willard pointed out to the critic Katherine Kuh that Smith considered the medals to be drawings rather than "actual work" (that is, sculpture).

With the *Medals* the frame of a work became important to Smith for the first time. He used ovals, circles, and squares with clipped edges, varying in size from ten to sixteen inches. It was undoubtedly at Smith's behest that Willard, in her press release on the *Medals*, specifically pointed out how several elements break out of the frame in one medal, *Private Law and Order Leagues*. As also mentioned earlier, that idea can be traced back to 1930, when Smith adapted the idea of bleeding photographs off the page after having seen it done in a German magazine. In the 1950s, starting with *The Letter* Smith began systematically to violate the frames of his sculptures.

The conceptualization necessary in carving the *Medals* is the first precise indication of the beginning of Smith's major contribution to sculpture—his break with object making. The essence of sculpture had traditionally been the solid core, and it would continue to be for as long as sculptors carved or cast their forms. The solid core, of course, kept sculpture an art of objects. Elizabeth McCausland, documenting Smith's thoughts in 1940, wrote: "Conceptually the medals required a complete somersault. Direct carving cuts away the matrix, leaves the core. Reverse carving cuts away the core, leaves the matrix or mould. Instead of being outside working in on the subject, the sculptor had to imagine himself inside working out. He had to think of himself as inside the object space, cutting outward to the farthest edges to define the object."[13] Here we find the first evidence of Smith's thinking about a hollowed core, in this instance, literally carved out from solid material. If "frame" is substituted for "farthest edge," McCausland here exactly describes Smith's major interest during the last fifteen years of his career. During the 1940s the idea of cutting away the core remained with him, even though he became almost completely immersed in the creation of symbolic objects.

Smith originally intended the *Medals* to be shown at a gallery other than the Willard, but after a succession of rejections they were finally shown there in November 1940. None was sold, and by December Smith was so discouraged that he considered taking a teaching position. *Time, Newsweek,* and *The New Yorker* all published favorable articles on the series. Milton Brown wrote enthusiastically about it in *Parnassus.* (Several years later Brown sent the collector Joseph Hirshhorn to see the *Medals,* and Hirshhorn bought two of them and a small sculpture.) Howard Devree of the *New York Times* believed that the series ought to be assessed by a ''socio-historic interpreter'' rather than by an art critic.

Though they did not sell, enthusiasm over the *Medals* remained high for about a year. Alfred Barr expressed some interest in seeing them and thought he might use them if he ran an exhibition on the war. In spring 1941 they were sent to the Kalamazoo Institute of Art, where they were warmly received. Seven of the medals appeared at the American Artists' Congress Anti-War show on June 6 and 7, 1941, and in November of that year they went to the Walker Art Center. Several museum curators who were approached, however, were reluctant to show them for fear of their directors' disapproval of the controversial subject matter.

The outbreak of war on December 7, 1941, raised the possibility that the *Medals* would be considered antiwar propaganda because of their implication that there was little difference between the politically and economically powerful classes in America and those in totalitarian countries. When the United States entered the war, it became unpatriotic to protest against those charged with the nation's conduct, and Smith began to fear that the *Medals* might place him in an unfavorable light. In a letter to Marian Willard dated December 16, 1941, Smith began to change his position. ''I'm afraid everybody will misinterpret my point with the medallions—if shown again I'll insert an addenda specifically pointing to the fact that these are anti-fascist war medals.'' He added defensively, ''I haven't changed my thesis, the world has changed around me since 1938–39 when I worked the majority of them.''[14] In spring 1942 he had Marian Willard change the names of several medals to ''Aggressor-Acts'' and asked her to stop showing certain ones, such as the *Munition Makers,* which would be ''misunderstood.''[15] In a letter to J. D. Hatch, of the Albany Institute of History and Art,[16] Smith called the *Medals* an ''Axis-Devastation'' series depicting the ravagings of ''Japs and Fascists.'' Smith's proletarian convictions did not preclude efforts to turn his medallions into profit from the war effort. In a letter to the War Production Board in May 1942 he indicated that he could produce one hundred thousand medallions of ''superior artistic quality'' as rewards for productivity in defense factories.[17] Evidently still fearing that his *Medals* might be handicapping him, he emphasized that he intended his offer as a patriotic gesture. Once again he proclaimed the theme of the *Medals* to be antifascist and blamed the press for misreading them. In November 1942 Smith was still expressing anxiety that the *Medals* might be ''misinterpreted'' as appeasement.

5

THE WAR YEARS

The 1940s were years of gradually increased recognition for Smith. As previously mentioned, in 1938 he had been asked to serve as an alternate on the World's Fair Committee. In December 1939 the Sculpture Guild elected him to membership, through which he began to associate with William Zorach, José de Creeft, Paul Manship, and Robert Laurent, all of whom worked in monolithic form, the kind of art Smith so deeply resented. At the end of 1939 the Museum of Modern Art requested the loan of *Blue Construction,* which had been shown at the fair, for its sculpture garden. By 1943 Clement Greenberg could write in the *Nation* that if Smith could maintain his level of work, he would become one of America's greatest artists.[1] Other critics picked up the theme. In 1946 Milton Brown wrote in *Magazine of Art* that Smith was the "best sculptor in America."[2] Robert Cronbach's review of Smith's 1947 exhibition called it "smashing good" and Smith an extraordinary, genuine talent.[3] Just a few years earlier a writer had seen Smith's work as "miscellaneous plumbing that has survived a conflagation"[4] and another had called it "sewer pipe sculpture."[5]

During the same decade, however, an important personal change occurred in Smith. There may have been bitterness in his attitude during the 1930s, but it was offset by optimism for the future. Smith may at times have been extraordinarily naive, but his naivety saved him from despair. The 1940s, however, were years of reality. It was no longer romantic to be an artist, but hard, dirty work at real financial sacrifice. There were no more extravagant vacations. And it was no longer necessary to create a legend of himself as a workingman: Smith was to spend two long years in an armament factory. His way of surviving was to become as hard as the image he had earlier sought to project. By the end of the 1940s, there was no longer a separation between sculpture and life. Smith's existence was governed by the making of sculpture; all else became secondary. To succeed, Smith would do what was necessary.

An early step to be taken toward recognition was to make the Museum of Modern Art and Alfred Barr more aware of Smith the artist. The Modern was, during the 1930s and forties, by far the most prestigious American institution devoted to contemporary art. Its stamp of recognition offered honor as well as monetary rewards in the marketplace. There were, of course, degrees of recognition. In Smith's mind, the acquisition of a work for a modest sum was lowest on the scale; prestige rose in proportion to the amount paid. A one-man exhibition accorded the artist a "perfect score." With such a method Smith could know exactly where he stood in comparison with other artists, and to the highly ambitious Smith there was only one worthwhile position in the pecking order: "number-one boy," as he himself said.

For Smith to reach that lofty place, it was necessary to persuade Alfred Barr of his merits as an artist. Barr's position at the Modern during the late thirties and early forties seemed unassailable. He symbolized, both personally and professionally, the center of the powerful art circle that the young American abstractionists wished to penetrate. Fragile in appearance, cultured and erudite, Barr had been a Harvard professor before becoming the museum's director. He offered a considerable contrast to Smith's bulk, somewhat gruff demeanor, and pose as factory worker turned sculptor.

In Smith's quest for Barr's recognition, he surely was aided by Marian Willard's position as director of the museum's membership. Barr, however, was unenthusiastic about Smith's work; he felt it to be derivative of Joaquin Torres-Garcia.[6] Smith's attitude toward Barr was colored by his perception of Barr's judgment of his work. When he felt that Barr held it in relatively low esteem, Smith was angered. His behavior, which at times seemed incomprehensible to Barr, can be explained as a series of oblique movements calculated to gain attention.

Smith's first loyalty was to his work; if there were others, they were to fellow artists and family. To Smith and the other abstract artists of the thirties and forties, the galleries and museums were not collaborators in the advancement of art but enemies that had to be confronted and coerced into advancing the interests of artists.[7] There would always be a gulf between those who made art and those who did not. "Philosophers, historians, critics, museum directors can never help with our direction. Only artists know about art. They are the ones who make it, who really love it."[8] The events surrounding the purchase and repair of *Head* (1938; Fig. 23) by the Museum of Modern Art provide a clear example of Smith's ways of dealing with museums, and at the same time demonstrate why artists viewed museums as adversaries.

Smith produced *Head* when he was just beginning to be influenced by the World's Fair Trylon and Perisphere—and their shapes can be seen in *Head*'s profile. The forms were made of cast iron, drilled through, then strung on a steel rod like beads on a necklace. The use of cast iron in much of Smith's work during the first half of his career created considerable difficulties with museums and shipping companies. Cast iron shatters easily and cannot be satisfactorily welded. At least six or seven of Smith's cast-iron sculptures were broken in transit. Smith blamed the museums, the packers, the shippers—never his choice of material. For two years after *Iron Woman* was damaged in 1956 en route from the Whitney Museum back to Bolton Landing, Smith remained unreconciled with the museum.

Alfred Barr first requested the loan of *Head* for the Museum of Modern Art's sculpture garden in early 1941, with the understanding that it might be purchased when funds became available. Whether he really liked *Head* very much is a matter of doubt. Marian Willard believed it was the only Smith work Barr did like,[9] but the art critic Thomas Hess felt it was

Fig. 23. *Head,* 1938. Cast iron and steel. 19¾ × 9⅝″. Collection and photo courtesy The Museum of Modern Art, New York. Gift of Charles E. Merrill

a matter of balancing the museum's collection of European metal sculptors with an example of American abstraction.[10] As late as 1956 Smith referred to Barr's dislike of his work (and claimed he did not care).[11]

In May 1943 *Head* was sold to the museum for $300, and Marian Willard wrote in relief, "Here endeth our first bout with them."[12] A difficult situation arose, however, when Barr ordered Dorothy Miller, then his assistant and later curator of the museum collections, to obtain a 10 percent museum discount. Willard, pointing out that the money for the purchase came from a donation rather than directly out of museum funds, declined to give the discount. The petty haggling clouded Smith's pleasure in this first sale to a major institution, and annoyance turned to anger when Smith learned that he had received less than the full amount set aside for the purchase. Charles Merrill had donated funds to purchase both the Smith work and one by another artist at a cost of either $450 or $500 each. The Modern's withholding of money set aside for the purchase of his sculpture reinforced Smith's conviction that museums' interests ran counter to those of artists.

The opportunity to even accounts came in mid-July 1944, when several sailors on shore leave accidentally knocked down *Head,* bending the rod on which the modular forms had been strung and chipping some of the cast forms. The museum asked Smith how much he would charge to repair it. Smith said he would do the work for $150—a sum that when coupled with the purchase price would equal the original amount to which he felt entitled. Since the damage was minor, the museum rejected his estimate and decided to obtain others. Smith effectively blocked that effort by threatening to obtain an injunction. "I do not consider that the sculpture in its present condition is worthy of exhibition," he wrote. "Nobody but the sculptor is competent to make repairs."[13] In August Smith threatened to bring his case before the United Steelworkers Union, to which he then belonged. At the beginning of September the museum capitulated.

The museum's reasons for finally agreeing to Smith's price seem clear. The costs in time, adverse publicity, and perhaps legal fees far outweighed any possible savings in repair costs. More important still may have been Smith's threat to disown the sculpture. Museums continually repair and restore works of art. Any time a work is touched by an artisan, the original is necessarily altered. In this instance, repairs might not have been noticed even by Smith. If the museum had been forced publicly to accept his statement that only the sculptor is competent to repair his work, restoration and repair of work of living artists could be opened to question. It is apparent that Smith did not really believe his own words. Though he preferred to make his own repairs, he occasionally was content to advise the owner as to how the repair should be done. His real discovery was that the threat of publicly airing a controversy might be turned to his advantage. As we shall see, Smith would make use of that knowledge.

The bombing of Pearl Harbor in December 1941 raised a barrier in the path of Smith's career and forced a drastic reduction in his output of work. Several days after the bombing, Marian Willard wrote glumly that with America's entry into the war, the nation's new priorities would make the sale of sculpture even more difficult than it ordinarily was, and she advised Smith to find employment that could tide him over until the war's end. The uncertainty caused by the war, the difficulty of obtaining materials, and low sales of sculpture persuaded Smith to take Willard's advice and seek employment. Fear of army discipline led him to look for a position in which he would be exempt from the draft. As early as 1940 he had expressed the fear that being drafted into the army would ''ruin'' him and his work.[14] He first volunteered his services to design a defense-school emblem that could serve as a national insignia. A few days later, in May 1942, he made his offer to produce up to one hundred thousand medallions for the War Production Board—a highly optimistic figure since his only relevant experience was the production of the fifteen *Medals for Dishonor*, a project that had taken him several years. On June 1 he wrote to American Locomotive in Schenectady, New York, in regard to a job in the design department, citing his work in his own shop, which specialized, he said, in architectural and museum work. Efforts to obtain a job in Washington through the aid of friends failed, as did all of his other attempts to avoid factory work. Early 1942 found him in welding school, and by July he was welding armor plate on tank destroyers seven nights a week on the graveyard shift at American Locomotive. In August the Smiths closed up the farm and moved into the attic of a house in Schenectady.

Smith's later reputation as an exceptionally hard-working sculptor can be traced to the conditioning he underwent in adapting to factory work. In meeting war production needs, Smith had to learn to work irregular hours and tolerate the monotony and hard work of assembly-line production. In the first few weeks he lost fifteen pounds. Yet it was the mental strain that seemed more serious. Though he became a first-rate welder, earning three raises in three months, Smith, to Dorothy's great concern, did not talk about either his work or his fellow workers. The discipline of factory work chafed but Smith did not leave, probably for fear of the draft. The need to make money for future shop expansion could have been another reason.

The factory years were much more than just an interruption of Smith's sculpture career. They forced him into dealing with the realities of earning a living, and the experience was not pleasant. For the first time Smith could not leave a position at his own pleasure, a different situation certainly from the summer job of 1925 at the Studebaker factory, from which he knew he would return to college. Neither would there be an opportunity to take several extra weeks of vacation as he had done at the Furlong farm, nor to quit the job for a nine-month visit to the Virgin Islands or to take an extended tour of Europe.

The sale of *Head* in May 1943 helped to sustain hope of a way eventually to escape factory work. In that same month Smith wrote Marian Willard that it was time to gamble on selling his art work. He seemed, however, to need approval of the decision from his wife: ''Dottie and I talked it over. She backs me in the stand that I shouldn't work on anything but my own sculpture. I'm 37, life is short, I've worked at dozens of jobs trying to be an artist—from now on we sink or swim on my chosen profession. . . . Its time to do what we want. Dot says so.''[15]

His first serious work experience had drastically and permanently changed Smith. He was no longer merely imitating the life of a factory worker, and it had been a rude awakening. With that experience came an exterior toughness and bitterness that would be reflected in the sculptures of the post-factory era, particularly in the "Spectre" series, including *Perfidious Albion, Figure of Greed, False Peace Spectre, The Rape, Pillar of Sunday, Spectre Riding the Golden Ass,* and *Spectre of Mother,* all of which were constructed in or about 1945.

Though he had turned bitter, Smith had become his own man. In July 1944, though no longer at American Locomotive, and at the time of the dispute with Alfred Barr over the repair of *Head,* Smith could write to Marian Willard of his plans without using the word "we" or needing permission. His hard factory experiences had knocked the naiveté forever out of him and given him a strength and a pride that Smith had previously lacked. He planned to be more direct about what he wanted in life: "Maybe I'm getting hard and cynical but my factory period gave me long periods to think and certainly changed many values. From now on, I don't wear gloves. . . . If I run out of or low on funds, I'll go back to the factory before I'll sacrifice my ideals or my art and the market. While I consider my work has had some success d'estime, I haven't had success d'cashine and I'm not sure where the line can be drawn."[16]

During his two years at American Locomotive Smith had saved a substantial amount of money, so he could now start to seek "success d'cashine." But the years at the factory had been difficult for Smith, and his relationship with Dorothy had changed as his isolation grew. They separated in 1945 and then were reconciled a few months later. During the 1940s they underwent even greater stress that the marriage did not survive.

The war had drastically affected Smith's sculpture production. Metals were obtainable only for war-related uses, and his hours at the factory were so long that the Smiths could drive to Bolton Landing only when he began to have weekends off. Obtaining oxygen and acetylene for welding and gasoline to travel to Bolton Landing presented other problems, but still Smith persevered. Typically, after finishing a swing shift on Saturday morning and with a free Sunday, the Smiths would drive straight to the farm from the factory, enabling Smith to have as much time as possible for his sculpture. He became resourceful in finding materials. With metal unavailable, he began to work with marble at Mallery and LaBrake, a monument manufacturer in Saratoga Springs, using their power tools rather than the traditional hammer and chisel. He was again demonstrating the preference for mechanical tools which made him a truly twentieth-century sculptor.

The war, however, was not the only impediment to sales; a preoccupation with Surrealism was also having an effect. Willard wrote in early 1942 that "the art world is overpowered at the moment by Surrealists . . . but real art is simmering below the surface."[17] By "real art" she clearly was referring to abstraction. It is not difficult, however, to see Smith's embracing of a highly figurative symbolism during the 1940s as related to that trend.

Smith's experiences in making the *Medals for Dishonor* had aroused his interest in casting, a process that made possible the release of those fantastic forms and figures that teemed in his mind. The plasticity of wax enables it to accept extraordinary nuances of form. Images could emerge in the wax and eventually, of course, in metal, just as Smith had imagined them. His work with welded steel was essentially a process of joining parts already formed; cast forms produce a vastly different type of art.

In 1940, having studied a book on the subject by Malvina Hoffman, Smith began to experiment with casting, using the lost-wax method. For this technique a wax model is usually made, then covered with a heat-resistant material called the "investment." The investment subsequently becomes the mold for the molten metal, which is poured into the cavity created after the wax has been burned out in a kiln. During the "pour," ventilation back to the surface must be provided so that air and gases do not become trapped and prevent the metal from flowing to all parts of the cavity.

Smith's first work done by this method is *Untitled*, a bronze (1940; Fig. 24) of Dorothy Dehner bathing in a wheelbarrow. The wax model had been burned out in the Smiths' kitchen oven, causing thick smoke to fill the house. The heat had been insufficient to burn out all of the wax, and improper venting had kept the metal from flowing through some of the linear sections. As a result, several breaks occurred which had to be welded together. The horizontal strips on either side of the figure were evidently to serve as runners to carry the metal throughout the figure. Rather than removing them, Smith kept them as part of the sculpture—an unorthodox idea.

Smith painstakingly persevered at learning how to gate and vent his models until he mastered the technique. (By late August 1940, displaying his characteristic enthusiasm, he was planning to make a hundred castings.) In the process, even failures were turned to advantage. When his casts were unsuccessful and he had to repair broken forms by welding, Smith made the makeshift technique part of his art. He continued to use welding in combination with cast forms, and in time used both methods equally in his works. *Perfidious Albion*, for example, (1945; Fig. 25) was cast three times; each casting was turned into an original work by the addition of welded parts.

A rather strange little sculpture, *Widow's Lament* (1942–43; Fig. 26), demonstrates Smith's imaginative combining of welding and casting and is important as an indication of the direction his work would take during the late 1940s and well into the 1950s. The frame has been cast in bronze, almost surely not because of that metal's artistic associations but because of the difficulty of casting steel. The solid metal frame for the figure was most practically formed by casting; the building up of layers of rod by means of welding would have been costly in both time and material. Having cast his frame, Smith then went to work with his torch to develop the forms it would enclose. Welding permitted him to improvise and alter; it gave him a flexibility denied to the artist who receives his form back from the foundry in a condition that permits almost no further aesthetic input. With two large feet firmly planted on the ground and curled, earlike elements at the sides of the frame, this little anthropomorphic figure has elements of humor and intimacy which are quite compelling. A look back at *Structure of Arches* (Fig. 19), *Medals for Dishonor* (Fig. 21), and *Interior for Exterior* (Fig. 16), all from 1939, and *Interior* (Fig. 13), from 1937, serves to remind us what a wide range of styles Smith was capable of working in and how very eccentric his work was.

Fig. 24. *Untitled (Dorothy Dehner Bathing in Wheelbarrow)*, 1940. Bronze. 5 × 5⅛ × 3½″. Collection Dorothy Dehner, New York. Photo by Stanley E. Marcus

70

Fig. 25. *Perfidious Albion,* 1945. Bronze, steel. 14⅜ × 4½ × 2⅝″. Collection Dorothy Dehner, New York. Photo by David Smith

Fig. 26. *Widow's Lament,* 1942–43. Forged and fabricated steel and bronze. 13½ × 20 × 6⅝″. Private collection. Photo courtesy collection

It is the *Widow*'s frame and the boxes within it which best remind us of the element of continuity in Smith's work: he liked to act out dramas through his sculptures. For example, the pedestal of *Structure of Arches*, as we have seen, functions as a stage for imagery, which puts the viewer in the position of voyeur of a scene of sexual menace. In *Widow*'s *Lament*, each box contains a separate event, labeled by Smith, from left to right, "simplicities of childhood," "knots of adolescence," "complexities of marriage," and "sorrow."[18] The work itself is based on the death of Smith's father several years earlier. Though he had used frames before, *Widow's Lament* foreshadows the way Smith used them during the early 1950s. When we compare *Widow's Lament* with *The Letter* (1950; Fig. 27) we see that each uses a frame to encompass a number of smaller frames. The inner frames of both works function much as the pedestal in *Structure of Arches:* both serve to define the boundaries of areas on which the viewer's attention is to be focused. There are major differences, however, between *Widow* and *Letter,* on the one hand, and, on the other, *Structure* and the early Giacomettis on which it was based. Smith had taken a highly innovative step in *Widow's Lament* and *The Letter* by structuring them vertically, thus enabling them to accommodate multiple events *within* the surface, rather than atop it, as in *Structure*. Each of the several events in *Widow* and *Letter* is self-contained and exists as a separate focal area, anticipating the time when Smith would use found objects within frames in the same manner.

Interesting parallels may also be drawn between the two vertical works, *Widow's Lament* and *The Letter,* and the horizontally based *Home of the Welder* (see Figs. 14, 15). *Home,* despite its pedestal/stage, is essentially a vertical sculpture because most of its forms are intended to be seen vertically, against the room walls. Yet to see all components, the viewer is compelled to walk around it, as with traditional sculpture. A peripatetic view, however, is not wholly illuminating because of the impenetrable compartments that split *Home* into independent segments. Hence Smith's logic in eventually flattening his structures becomes apparent. *Home* exists more as three separate vertical structures than as an entity resting on a pedestal. Both *Widow* and *Letter* appear more effective sculpturally, thanks to vertical formats, which expose all segments at once and so avoid the fragmentation of *Home of the Welder*.

Smith's creation of pedestal dramas, called by Edward Fry "table-top tableaux,"[19] reached its peak during 1945 and 1946 before tapering off and ending with *Sacrifice* in 1951. Several major characteristics of those works can be defined. All involve miniature dramas or scenes, pedestal/stages, interaction among discrete forms (as opposed to monolithism), and symbolism or imagery, often autobiographical. As in the earlier *Structure of Arches*, whose forms both recall their source in the World's Fair buildings and create a scene of sexual menace, the imagery operates on several levels. The use of the pyramidal form as a female symbol also derives from *Structure of Arches*.

Smith carried out his most extensive symbolism in *Home of the Welder*. Here, as in other works, he laid a trap for critics by using extremely simplistic symbols (millstone, ball and chain) in a realistic miniature setting and combining them with other recondite ones. In joining the obvious to the abstruse, Smith created a temptation to view *Home of the Welder*

Fig. 27. *The Letter,* 1950. Welded steel. 37⅝ × 22⅞ × 9¼″. Collection and photo courtesy Munson-Williams-Proctor Institute, Utica, New York

as a puzzle to be deciphered. But such an effort is quite likely to be defeated. Smith more often than not revealed in order to conceal.

An early discussion of *Home of the Welder* appeared in 1957 in the introduction to the catalogue of Smith's first major exhibition at the Museum of Modern Art. Although the essay was written by Sam Hunter, then associate curator of the Modern's Department of Painting and Sculpture, the work's symbolism is explained so specifically that the information could have been supplied only by Smith himself. The essay states that *Home of the Welder* is intended to depict the life of a "fellow welder," though the work is obviously autobiographical, as previously noted by Edward Fry. "Fellow welder" seems to have been used to disguise thinly Smith's apparent unhappiness with the state of his own marriage. At one point in the essay, the wife is pictured as Medusa; at another, according to Hunter's interpretation, she metamorphoses into a predaceous plant. The wheel and chain symbolize the welder's burdens, and a small bronze duck symbolizes "his fantasies of owning a game preserve in the country." A "double-profile reindeer" is framed on the wall. (Smith was an ardent hunter; during times of financial hardship he shot his own supply of meat.) An undated letter to Marian Willard, written in a stream-of-consciousness style, offers further insight into Smith's imagery in regard to *Home of the Welder:* "Living room—Female pedestal on which grows a welder's dream flower. A millstone hangs around his neck related to his job. Duck sitting on a cushion—a welder's idea. Dumbells—Paintings and drawings made by the Welder in his room in locomotive works. Woman and jackass. Top of room—a head projecting from frame picture. Otherside—Welder's wife in the bedroom in front of a big mirror. Angular locomotive—A woman made of locomotive parts, looking in mirror is a glamorous vision of himself."[20]

By 1945 Smith was more concerned with imagery than he ever would be again. By that time, repetition of certain symbols made their meanings clear. The derivation of *Egyptian Landscape* (see Fig. 18) from the architectural symbols of the World's Fair has already been discussed. *The Rape* (1945; Fig. 28), made several years before *Landscape*, involves those same symbols. The *V* of the Trylon is translated into the sprawl of the woman's legs. The relationship of the Perisphere to the cannon becomes clear if we remember Smith's predilection for vulgar language. The Perisphere is a ball; the two cannon wheels, as two-dimensional counterparts of the ball, indicate two "balls" (or testicles). The cannon (which fascinated Smith since childhood) works exceedingly well as a male symbol. Smith also used the bird as another symbol of the phallus, here combining images by mounting a pair of folded wings on the cannon barrel. It is the head of the bird, however, that he found particularly attractive as a symbol, since it combines a round form with a pointed triangular beak (again the World's Fair symbols). The form can be read clearly in *Egyptian Landscape* as both genitalia and bird's head. One of Smith's favorite slang terms was "peckerhead" to describe someone who had his "pecker" where there should have been a brain. In 1945 Smith made at least four bird sculptures, including two of cockfights ("cock," of course, being another word for "penis.") Much of Smith's imagery contains sexual ambiguity as well. The implication of homosexuality which can be read in the word "cockfight" ought not to be overlooked. It can be noted also that in *Cockfight—Variation*

Fig. 28. *The Rape,* 1945. Bronze. 9 × 5⅜ × 3½″. Collection Stephen D. Paine, Boston. Photo by David Smith

76

Fig. 29. *Cockfight—Variation,* 1945. Steel. 34″ on steel base. Collection and photo courtesy Whitney Museum of American Art, New York. Photo by Geoffrey Clements

(1945; Fig. 29) all of the beaks are open. We have seen that the *V* shape is characteristic of Smith's female forms as well, and that the pyramidal form frequently symbolized the female breast to Smith.

The private symbolism of particular forms is, however, of less significance than what began to occur with the repetition of these forms. When simplified and repeated in series of works, certain forms were lifted out of the realm of the strictly personal and could begin to function independently of their private meanings. The transformation was made explicit in the 1950s, when Smith named his first major series the ''Tanktotems.'' For by combining the form (tank lids) with the subject matter (totemism) in the title, Smith was announcing their equal significance in the work.

6

GROWING ISOLATION AND THE SEARCH FOR A NEW IDENTITY

The Smiths had originally intended to use the farmhouse at Bolton Landing as a weekend residence. Without insulation or electricity, with a small coal stove for heat and an outside hand pump for water, the farm was a strenuous place to live during upstate New York winters. The first addition, which they made in the early 1930s, was a small dirt-floored shed that Smith used for a workshop. In 1937 it was replaced by a larger cinder-block shop.

At the end of David's work for the WPA in 1939, the Smiths decided to move permanently to Bolton Landing and live as much as possible off the land, in the hope that by doing so they could stretch Dorothy's small income to permit David to devote full time to his sculpture. They raised their own vegetables and livestock, which Smith learned to butcher, and shot game. (Once Dorothy sautéed and pickled a tree fungus that David found.) Though Smith's shop was quite snug, the house, now more than a hundred years old, remained unaltered. Gaps were beginning to appear between its planks. During the winters, temperatures could drop to 30 degrees below zero.

Although they were able, despite gasoline rationing, regularly to weekend in Bolton Landing, work on the farm did not commence until the end of Smith's work at the armament factory. The Smiths returned to Bolton Landing in September 1944 with substantial savings from David's work. Dorothy dreaded the coming winter, but a letter to Edgar Levy indicates that despite her misgivings, David was determined to remain. By January the farm would be lonesome and cold.[1] But the winter would not prevent Smith from making sculpture. The shop had a concrete floor and sufficient heat to enable him to work in the coldest weather. In November he bought an electric welder and installed a foundry.

In July 1945 Dorothy left David, going to stay in New York. David later followed and the two remained there until both returned to the farm in late March or early April. (It was during this time Smith made *Home of the Welder*.) By the following October they had decided to build a new house and were accumulating materials for it. For some reason, Smith did not want anyone to know of their plans; this was to be, Dorothy noted, "another Smith secret."[2] Smith's isolation, first apparent at American Locomotive, was now being fostered by his relentless will to work and the harsh winters.

The new house was to have no frills. It was to be a "cheap utility model. . . ."[3] Perhaps in consideration of future tax assessments, Smith described it as a research building with living quarters. Since the basement and garage were to be used for mixing chemicals and printmaking and a portion of the upstairs was to be a painting studio, the description seems accurate. The building was to be of cinder blocks, with floor and roof of steel. Smith would be his own contractor and do most of the labor, and Dorothy would do much of the rest. Radiant heat was to emanate from the ceiling according to a plan drawn up by James Fitch, an architect and close friend. The old house had been built on the site commanding the best view on the property, a vista that reached to Lake George. The new one was to occupy the same site. Since the Smiths had to live in the old house while building was going on, it was moved and the new one erected on the site. The funds came in part from Dorothy's inheritance, a loan from Marian Willard, Smith's earnings from American Locomotive, and the sale of trees for lumber. Sales of sculpture at Smith's 1946 and 1947 Willard Gallery exhibitions added to the fund, after a considerable portion was used for shop equipment (including a cutoff saw at a cost of over three thousand dollars.)[4]

Construction of the house finally began in March 1947 and took over two years. When the old house was being moved it had fallen off the jacks, opening additional gaps in the walls. By October, Smith was resenting the time the house was diverting from his sculpture. At Christmas funds were low; all of their money was going into the house. Even their diet was restricted. The pump did not work, and on occasion they had to melt snow to make water for washing; drinking water was obtained from a nearby spring. In November 1947 Marian Willard sent them a thousand dollars, which Smith was to consider a loan, an advance, or whatever he liked. In February 1948 she sent an electric blanket (they now had electricity), which together with a heating pad during the day kept Dorothy reasonably warm. David, calculating the electricity for the blanket alone at two dollars a month, was resentful of the cost.

The Smiths had to stop work on the house during the winter because of the intense cold, and they still had not resumed it by May. A position as instructor became available at Sarah Lawrence College, in Bronxville, New York, and Smith was recommended for it by Theodore Roszak. Smith rejected the first offer; the salary, he said, was too low. Smith was growing increasingly short-tempered. When, in June, he was finally ready to resume work, all of his potential helpers had found summer jobs. Thus it fell to Dorothy to scrape and paint the steel beams that were out in the meadow and intended for the floor. In July the roof went up, after Smith ingeniously rigged a steel cart on tracks, powered by the truck motor to carry materials to the top of the house. Dorothy described the house as like a Smith sculpture: "crafted and finished and strong to a fare thee well."[5] Work on the house during the summer of 1948 precluded work on sculpture. In September, just as the shortage of money was becoming acute, a sculpture was sold and Sarah Lawrence raised its salary offer. This time Smith accepted the job.

In January 1949 the Smiths were still living in the "old wreck" with no heat. All stoves had been put in the new house in an attempt to dry out the ceiling plaster. Inside the old one, temperatures dropped to 24 degrees. That winter was the coldest in Bolton Landing since 1882. It was not until June 1949 that the Smiths finally moved into their new house.

Life, during the construction of the house, may be perceived as harsh to many of us.

According to Dorothy Dehner, however, she and Smith saw this part of their lives as a kind of grand adventure. There were frequent moments of tenderness and serenity. Humor relieved some of the more stressful events. Living close to the soil made for an enriched feeling for life. Though the time may have seemed difficult, Dorothy Dehner remembers it as a time of particular closeness to her husband.

The Smiths' marriage, however, did not survive long past the completion of the house. Smith's violent temperament grew over the years and Dorothy became unable to cope with it. On Thanksgiving day 1950, she left. When Dorothy sued for divorce, Smith seemed to feel genuine remorse over the way he had treated her. He wrote her, "If I cannot pay the life, I'll try at least to pay the dollars."[6] The final agreement called for no alimony, merely repayment of some of the money Dorothy had put into the house. It was to have been repaid within ten years, but Smith, who seemed determined on a new start, repaid the debt in half that time. He then closed off another part of his life by going to the Levys and telling them, "I'm leaving you to Dorothy."[7]

Behind Smith's self-imposed isolation lay the determination to forge a new image. Both his professional and personal lives were affected. Just as Smith had always been reticent about his childhood and parents, his pattern of cutting off his past now was being repeated; and his future was to begin with a new wife. In 1949 Smith had met Jean Freas at Sarah Lawrence. Jean was very different from Dorothy, who was several years older than Smith and had frequently been his tutor in the arts and other areas. Jean, twenty-three years younger than Smith, was much taken with the burly artist in his tweed suit and cap, who taught drawing, insisting on freedom and action through use of the entire arm. An erratic courtship began during 1949 and 1950, Smith's second year at the college, marred by a number of arguments (which stemmed from Smith's jealousy).[8] During the courtship Smith signed "Freeman" to some of his letters to Jean—a reference perhaps to his divorce but more likely to the new life he was carving.

In late 1952 David Durst, chairman of the art department at the University of Arkansas in Fayetteville, offered Smith the position of visiting artist, with use of a private studio, for the spring term of 1953. Smith accepted but was plagued by loneliness and begged Jean to join him. The two were married on April 6, 1953, in a feed-and-grain store, among bags of grain that Smith saw as fertility symbols, with Edward Millman (like Smith, a visiting professor at Arkansas) and his wife, Norma, as witnesses.[9]

The basis of Smith's change of professional image lay in his awareness of his growing reputation as a sculptor. He responded as he had during his American Locomotive experience: there would be more toughness in his demands and greater insistence on "success d'cashine." He began to exhibit some of that "defensive belligerence" that he had insisted was necessary. His dealer, Marian Willard, was to be strongly affected by the new attitude.

Already in 1946 some artists and critics were judging Smith the best sculptor in America. Monitoring the careers of other sculptors with growing confidence, Smith was pleased to discover that his own 1946 exhibition at the Willard Gallery had produced over twice as many sales as Jacques Lipchitz's. The sale of *Cockfight—Variation* to the Whitney Museum, also in 1946, did not entirely please him, however, even though the Whitney paid a much higher price than the Modern had paid for *Head*. For the first time, Smith repri- manded Willard, demanding to know who was responsible for giving the Whitney its "bargain." The price paid by Joseph Hirshhorn for three *Dishonor* medals and a small sculpture also seemed too low to Smith. And he was extremely dissatisfied with his 1947 Willard exhibition, particularly its catalogue.

> Reproduction seems to sell work and introduce it to out of town people who don't see the show. Reproductions stick in files, libraries—and make contact in people's minds so when they do get to New York they already know the work in part. Reproduction seems to act as first acquaintance and eliminate some of the barriers. In our case, acquisitions come from repeated showing. I just think reproduction helps the acquaintance and acquisition.[10]

Smith felt that Willard should have advertised the show more widely. He claimed that critics did not receive announcements on time. When Willard proposed to show some of Smith's works in the back office because he had delivered more than could be displayed to advantage in the gallery, he stormed that he would not permit his work to be "slighted." Before another exhibition, he wrote Willard that they would have to come to an agreement on the precise nature of their obligations.

The time had come for Smith to begin to assume control over the treatment of his work. His self-esteem was becoming inseparable from his work, and both were measured by the prices he could command in the marketplace. Marian Willard landed a four-day stint for Smith as juror at a museum in Minneapolis. Although he was hard-pressed for money at the time, Smith demanded four times the pay that had been offered. Smith's apparent ar- rogance in fact illuminated the core of the problem artists had in dealing with museums. With justification, Smith pointed out that he could earn more money as a welder. Why was it, he asked, that museums could manage to pay janitors and publicity people but not artists? Esteem was not enough; artists needed the "cashine" too. The pressure for money and the long hours of work with little financial reward could cause even someone as determined as Smith to wonder if it was all worthwhile. In early May 1948 he wrote Marian Willard:

> I'm in a soft mood. Having just lost face a couple times lately with bankers, etc.—and I start to look over my last year. Is my work slipping, does my boorishness, etc., chase people away? Am I overpriced? It just seems to me that I am somewhat responsible for my poor showing despite the compliments from critics this year. I start in everything, like its a battle, even battles don't occur that often. I start to battle before I know if there is an opponent. I find it awfully hard to fit in with my world. I get very lonesome (we) up here alone. Yet the dives and conditions in Brooklyn sort of drove me up here. I don't think I hit these lows when I'm more successful and doing my own work.
>
> Been trying to pick up a few bucks welding lately. Will start on the house soon and then I'll be too engrossed to ponder. . . . Did you promote the Minneapolis project and did I show ingratitude by raising the ante? I guess it was a cross between union standards and pride. I'm sorry I gummed the works.[11]

It is possible to see connections between the direction Smith's sculpture took and the course of his life. Much of the early work had an openness that reflected the ingenuousness of the "Aunt Flo" letters. His anger toward the turbulent, unjust world of the late 1930s found its outlet in the *Medals for Dishonor*. Feelings about his wife and his mother were almost directly translated into his work. His bitterness in the mid-1940s turned into the "Spectre" series. But gradually a change took place. In the late 1940s Smith began to renew professional acquaintances and meet other artists and critics who saw art not as a catharsis but as a mode of expression which transcended the artist's own personal experiences. Brought together by this determination to distinguish between art and experience, these artists were known simply as the New York Group. Smith's work began to move away from his personal, naive style of the mid-forties. In order to grow, he needed contact with artists who were exchanging ideas.

One important new avenue of access to this exchange was provided by the annual Woodstock conferences, the first beginning in late August 1947. Woodstock, in the Catskill Mountains of New York, had attracted artists for many years. In 1930 Juliana Force, director of the Whitney Studio Club and the new Whitney Museum of American Art, went there and spent a considerable sum for works by artists made destitute by the Depression.[12] These works helped form the collection of the Whitney Museum, which opened its doors to the public on November 18, 1931. Smith, realizing that the isolation of Bolton Landing had cut him off from the ferment of ideas, found in the Woodstock conference a way of keeping in touch with fellow artists, critics, and museum representatives.

The first conference, however, was traumatic for Smith, as it brought him into open conflict with a woman of considerable stature in the art world—precisely the sort of woman who represented the authority with which he had never learned to cope. The theme of the conference was the relationship of the artist to the museum. The museum's viewpoint was represented by the staff of the Whitney and Juliana Force, then in her seventies and the last year of her life. Smith, whose difficulties with museums were well known, was invited to speak for the sculptors. Herman Cherry, chairman of the Woodstock Education Committee, evidently had not met Smith at the time he extended the invitation;[13] later he became Smith's closest friend and confidant.

Smith's speech dealt with the financial and other difficulties sculptors have in their relationships with museums,[14] and was devoted in part to the inequity of the museums' practice of deducting a commission from the purchase price when they acquired a work of art. Unfortunately, Smith also brought up state sponsorship of art, a subject in which he was less knowledgeable. Juliana Force asked if the recent defeat of a legislative bill to establish a New York State art program could be attributed to the public's failure to understand the bill's intent. Smith, unaware of the bill and misunderstanding the question, suggested that such a bill should be introduced. Force criticized him sharply for his ignorance of the terms, provisions, and history of a bill with which he should have been deeply concerned. She pointed out that it had failed twice—a fate that was hardly surprising if artists themselves took so little interest in it.[15] Smith could only confess his ignorance and plead that he would rather be judged for his work than for his memory.[16]

83

The incident preyed on his mind. In October Smith wrote to Herman Cherry that he had answered badly and would like to change his response for the transcript of the conference proceedings, which was intended for publication.[17] He wrote an apology to Juliana Force, explaining that he did not speak well extemporaneously.[18] Still he could not let the matter rest. He wrote to Hudson Walker, executive director of Artists' Equity, that his answer had been tangled and that he wanted the transcript to be edited as if no questions had been asked.[19] In January he wrote to Walker again to make sure that the dialogue had been edited to conceal his confession of ignorance.[20]

Smith's acquaintance with Herman Cherry also gave him another way of maintaining contact with the New York Group. Cherry recognized Smith's need and made his Greenwich Village apartment available to him on Smith's monthly trips to New York City. Cherry was among the first to take Smith to gatherings at the Artists' Club (later the Eighth Street Club) and the Cedar Street Tavern. Smith had known the Group since the days when it congregated at the Waldorf Cafeteria, before the war. The move to Bolton Landing in 1940 and then to Schenectady had prevented him from maintaining his early associations. Friendship with Clement Greenberg, the art critic who was Smith's first important advocate, renewed those contacts, but it was having access to Herman Cherry's apartment which enabled Smith to attend the gatherings irregularly. The formation of Artists' Equity in 1947 by Yasuo Kuniyoshi found Smith, always interested in union causes, a willing member of the board of governors. Smith now became as much a part of the New York Group as his feelings of isolation would permit.

Probably reflecting the influence of the painters in the New York Group, Smith's work became more vertically oriented in the late 1940s. There was also a return to the linearity of the mid-thirties, though it was now more gestural. At the same time the heavy load of symbolism began to lighten.

Though *Oculus* (Fig. 30), made in 1947, retains some of the earlier symbolism, it has a columnar pedestal rather than the flat one characteristic of the mid-1940s work. Its elements rise vertically on a relatively flat plane. The dominating bulblike form is shaped from strips of steel that open up the interior volume, a contrast to the solid cast forms used in the mid-forties. Smith would continue to use cast forms, but they were losing their importance as he began to eschew the elaborate personal imagery for what would develop into a more public art during the 1950s and 1960s. The bird motif continued a while longer; in 1948 and 1949 Smith incorporated it into several works, such as *Eagle's Lair, The Eagle, Portrait of the Eagle's Keeper,* and *Royal Bird*—though not all of those works involved the sexuality of the symbol.

Smith's preoccupation with the Bolton Landing house and his job at Sarah Lawrence is reflected in the fact that he produced only three works in 1948 and seven in 1949, three of which were bronze castings. There were, however, two precedents of long periods of curtailed production being followed by great bursts of innovative energy. The first was his nine-month trip, from 1935 to 1936, to Europe, which decided his focus on sculpture and which inaugurated the prolific years of the late 1930s, when he produced his large body of linear works. The second hiatus occurred during World War II, after which Smith produced

Fig. 30. *Oculus*, 1947. Steel. 37 × 32½ × 10″ on wood base. Whereabouts unknown. Photo by David Smith

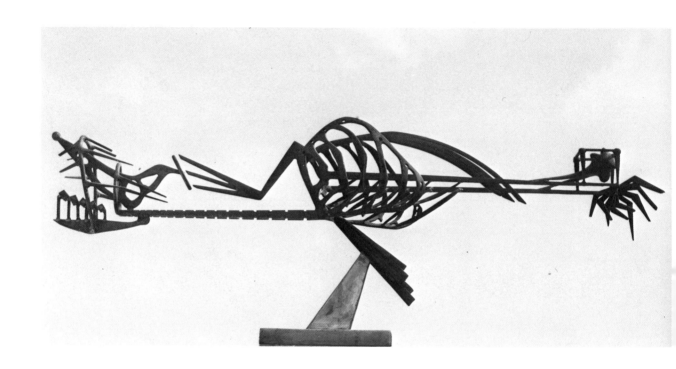

Fig. 31. *Royal Bird,* 1948. Welded steel, stainless steel. 21¾ × 59 × 9″. Collection Walker Art Center, Minneapolis. Gift of the T. B. Walker Foundation. Photo by David Smith

86

Fig. 32. *Australia,* 1951. Painted steel. 79½ × 107⅞″. Collection and photo courtesy The Museum of Modern Art, New York. Gift of William Rubin. Photo by Rudolph Burckhardt

the symbolistic works that first earned him his reputation as a serious artist. Both of those precedents were to pale, however, beside the revolution now brewing; at its conclusion, the art of sculpture had undergone a great change.

During the two years of limited production, only one significant work was made. *Royal Bird* (1948; Fig. 31) represents a continuation of Smith's interest in linear, insectile creatures, which he first created in the mid-1930s, continued with *Jurassic Bird* (1945), and then followed with *Australia* (1951; Fig. 32). *Royal Bird* shows Smith's abiding interest in strong horizontal lines on which to anchor his forms. Smith's observation of the way skeletons articulate space was turned into an ingenious composition using a horizontally placed bar to suggest a spinal column. Despite the symbolism still present in the elongated, sharply pointed triangular forms that link this work with the sculptures of the mid-1940s, *Royal Bird* evidences the renewal of a long-absent concern with formal composition. *Royal Bird* is based on a classic style of composition, with a focal area at each extremity of the implied central mass. The columnar pedestal, first seen in *Oculus*, has here been integrated in both form and material into the sculpture. Because their linear forms imply mass, both *Royal Bird* and *Jurassic Bird* have roots in the cast forms of the 1940s. A comparison of *Royal Bird* with *Australia* reveals how Smith refined these linear forms by 1951.

7

AN "IRASCIBLE" SCULPTOR

In 1950, twenty-two years after he had first applied for a Guggenheim fellowship[1]—or a "Guggie," as he called it—Smith's persistence was finally rewarded with the grant. The following year he won another. The two Guggenheim awards, coming at a time when he felt very discouraged and when his productivity had slackened, gave Smith a considerable boost. They helped pave the way for remarkable changes in his style and production, and Smith acknowledged their influence to the Guggenheim directors: "The first nine months to date have been the most fluent and productive period of my career."[2] It is possible that without some such tangible expression of approval, Smith might never have had the self-confidence to make radical changes.

One of the most important of the changes, and one immediately attributable to the awards, was the development of programmatic serializing of his sculptures. Though Smith had always tended to group works around central themes, now he seemed to think that his exact intentions had to be spelled out for the Guggenheim directors. His plans for the second year of the awards, he reported, included "5 works (steel) related to letter symbols (Greek Y's—18 h's, etc) . . . 10 works following poetic sculptural interpretations (such as the Forest, Star Cage, etc.) . . . 3 lost wax bronzes . . . 60, 19 × 25 drawings, studies for sculptural work . . . 14 steel plate etchings 12" × 14"–15"–16" in size."[3] Until the end of his career, Smith continued to group works based on a particular theme, and underlined the idea by giving each work in a series no other title than that of the theme itself followed by its number in the sequence: *Tanktotem I, Tanktotem II*, and so on.

The prestige of the Guggenheim fellowships helped to legitimize welding as a means of making art. Nevertheless, the directors betrayed their doubts by granting Smith his fellowships for "creative design in metals" rather than for sculpture. Despite Smith's growing prestige, the several museums that had acquired some of his small sculptures were content with their holdings, and collectors were still not buying his work. (Combined sales for 1949 and 1950 totaled about one thousand dollars.)[4] Welding had been granted a degree of respectability as an art form, but there was no evidence that the technique could itself sustain a major body of work. Before this time, Smith's work had comprised an amalgamation of techniques of which welding was only one. Combined techniques appeared necessary so long as Smith was borrowing from traditional sources rooted in biomorphic form. It was not until the 1950s, however, that Smith began systematically to explore the potential of welding alone and the possibility of establishing aesthetic principles indigenous to the new technique.

That Smith had once been primarily a painter and could therefore see beyond the conventional differences that separated painters from sculptors made it possible for him to act more readily in concert with goals of the New York Group. Also, the painters' determination for collective action, particularly through the newly established Artists' Equity, strongly appealed to Smith, who saw a united front of artists as the best defense against the museums' attempts to manipulate them individually. Yet Smith's ability to work as part of a group was severely limited. He remained essentially a loner. Wherever the New York painters met, in the Village, in Provincetown, in Woodstock, in Southampton, Smith prowled about on the fringes of the group, an onlooker rather than a participant. He would endorse their stands, then go his own way.

The New York Group had begun to use the news media to make their positions known and to enlist public support. The precedent for this sort of action was set when James Johnson Sweeney, director of the Department of Painting and Sculpture at the Modern, was asked to resign. His appointment in 1945 had aroused hope among the New York Group that what they perceived to be the museum's essentially negative policies toward them were about to change. Marian Willard expressed a view shared by many when she wrote to Smith that Sweeney's appointment would be a "breath of fresh air" and that "hope can rise again."[5] In late 1946 she had to report that the "same guys," Rene d'Harnoncourt, John Abbott, Alfred Barr, and their supporters were back in power and that Sweeney had resigned.[6] A letter of protest signed by Yasuo Kuniyoshi, Stuart Davis, Robert Motherwell, Jackson Pollock, I. Rice Pereira, and others was sent to the *New York Times*, but there is no evidence that it was effective. Smith was not among the signers, probably because his contact with the New York Group was still limited during that year before the first Woodstock conference.

The same action was taken again in 1950 against the Metropolitan Museum, which was being increasingly criticized for its failure to include any works of modern art among its collections. In response to the criticism, Francis Taylor, then the Metropolitan's director, had appointed Robert Beverly Hale as associate curator of American art in January 1949. Hale consulted Artists' Equity about ways in which the museum might be of assistance to its artists. Kuniyoshi, George Biddle, Henry Varnum Poor, Hudson Walker, and others responded that the most urgent need was for an open, competitive exhibition. Hale then proposed a national juried exhibition of American painting to be held in late autumn or winter of 1950. Entries were to be juried first in regional exhibitions, then in New York. In annual rotation there were to be similar exhibitions of sculpture, drawing, watercolors, and prints. It was clearly stipulated that the Metropolitan would be under no obligation to purchase any work; the growth of the museum's collection of American works was to have no connection with the exhibitions. That stipulation makes it seem as if the museum were concerned about being pressured into acquiring works it deemed inferior. Even more apparently defensive was the simultaneous announcement that an exhibition entitled "American Painters 1900–1950" would be held to show the "quality and depth" of the museum's collection, which Hale seemed compelled to defend: "A large and fairly representative exhibition of the painters of our period can be arranged from our collection as it now stands." To be included were academic painters of the turn of the century, such romantics as Ralph Blakelock and Albert Pinkham Ryder, the American Impressionists Mary Cassatt and Childe Hassam, academic portraiture from 1900 to 1950, and the most widely represented group, the "American Scene," plus the collection that Alfred Stieglitz had bequeathed to the museum. Hale conceded that "American painters inspired by the Armory Show" (the first major introduction of abstraction into the United States) had been omitted.[7] All of the categories listed by Hale for the exhibition had one aspect in common: they were figurative. There is not a single reference to "abstraction" in the museum *Bulletin* that carried the announcement. Hale's insistence that the Met's collection was representative of contemporary American art, coupled with his admission that it excluded artists influenced by the most important exhibition ever held in this country, only served to emphasize the collection's weakness.

In a gathering in May 1950 at Studio 35 on Eighth Street, the New York Group agreed to adopt Adolph Gottlieb's suggestion that they boycott the competition. An open letter to Roland L. Redmond, then president of the Metropolitan, was sent to the *New York Herald Tribune,* citing Taylor's publicly declared contempt for modern art and Hale's acceptance of a jury "hostile to advanced art" as the reasons for their refusal to submit works to the competition. As the first exhibition was to be of painting, the letter was signed by eighteen painters, among them Gottlieb, Robert Motherwell, William Baziotes, Hans Hofmann, Barnett Newman, Clyfford Still, Ad Reinhardt, Jackson Pollock, Mark Rothko, and Willem de Kooning. They were supported by ten sculptors, including Herbert Ferber, Ibram Lassaw, Day Schnabel, Seymour Lipton, Theodore Roszak, David Hare, Louise Bourgeois, and David Smith. Since the signers were members of Artists' Equity, whose leaders had originally proposed the competition, it is clear that there was a rift in that organization. A clue to its nature lies in the phrase "advanced art": it appears four times in the letter, and it is the only term used to describe the group's art. Nowhere does the term "abstract art" appear. It is safe to assume that the description "advanced" was intended to imply that the realists who had signed the original response to the museum were retrograde.

The letter may have gained publicity for the New York Group, but It failed to gain the *Herald Tribune*'s support. Dubbing the painters "The Irascible Eighteen," an editorial of May 23 stated: "One grows so accustomed to their irascibility that were it to cease one might well fear for their vitality." Irritated museum directors, the paper warned, might become immune to new ideas.

When the sculptors' turn to exhibit at the Metropolitan came, in 1951, the boycott was still in effect, and Ferber, Lipton, and Roszak all rejected invitations to become jurors—an honor that carried automatic acceptance of one work each. Smith, too, was invited to be a juror. And though he had signed the open letter in 1950 and later written Hudson Walker to urge a continuation of the boycott, he readily accepted. The group was displeased. There was talk of sending Smith a letter of protest, but Lassaw and Schnabel came to his defense, and there is no record of the letter being sent. Roszak wrote to Smith that despite his own refusal to serve, Smith's serving constituted "an acceptable jury of selection for me."[8] (Roszak did submit a work, which was accepted.) Smith rationalized his decision by saying he intended to "limber up" the unfounded prejudice of "self appointed guardians of the advanced position,"[9] but his choice left him with some strange bedfellows and deepened his sense of isolation. Fellow jurors were guardians of the monolithic sculptural tradition, who worked in either stone or cast bronze: Donal Hord, Robert Laurent, Hugo Robus, William Zorach, José de Creeft, Jacques Lipchitz.

In the foreword to the exhibition catalogue Hale wrote that only a small group of sculptors seemed to be working in a nonobjective style. The exhibition, however, was no basis for assessment. Of the ten sculptors who originally protested, only two—Smith and Roszak—had works on display; the others boycotted the exhibition. It is difficult to see, with the omission of Ferber, Lassaw, Lipton, Hare, and Bourgeois, on what grounds Smith made his statement before the Metropolitan Art Association in January 1952 that the selection was representative of contemporary American sculpture.[10]

Smith remained on the fringes of the New York Group and continued to feel isolated. In a sketchbook that he kept between 1950 and 1954 he wrote that he had acquaintances but no friends and suspected that he was unable to give what friends would demand. His sculpture took precedence over everything else. The real question, he thought, was why he had to measure his life by his work; there seemed to be nothing else in Smith's life. He suspected something of value had been lost.

His dedication, however, was beginning to achieve important results. In May 1953 an important milestone was passed: two "Tanktotems" were sold in one day. *Tanktotem I* (known as *Tanktotem Pouring*) was purchased by the Art Institute of Chicago, *Tanktotem II* (*Tanktotem Sounding*) by the Metropolitan. The fact that these are the only descriptively titled "Tanktotems" seems to indicate that they were at first named and only later, after Smith began to develop the series, given numbers.

Following these major sales, the Museum of Modern Art took steps finally to procure a recent work that would represent Smith in their collection more adequately than *Head* could do alone. Alfred Barr's effort, however, precipitated another clash. In June 1953, shortly after the Metropolitan and Art Institute purchases, Barr mentioned to Alfred Frankfurter, then editor and publisher of *Art News,* that in view of the Modern's limited budget, Smith would have a better chance of making a sale if he were prepared to reduce his prices. Frankfurter passed the information on to Smith through Thomas Hess, then managing editor of *Art News* and friendly with Smith.[11] Smith exploded. His anger was further fueled by the museum's purchase of two Reg Butler sculptures and a Richard Lippold.[12] In October he wrote to Dorothy Miller, curator of museum collections at the time, that he was prepared to buy back *Head* if for any reason the Modern was dissatisfied.[13] Meanwhile, Smith was having considerable difficulty collecting payment from the gallery (not the Willard) that had handled the sales to the Metropolitan and the Art Institute,[14] and there is little question that this problem exacerbated his agitation. Smith's offer to buy back *Head* was referred to the Committee on Museum Collections, which rejected it but said that if Smith felt the piece was not representative of his work, the committee would consider a partial exchange for a "later and more important example."[15] Smith answered in December that he would accept no "trade-ins" and went on to say that the maximum he would pay for *Head* was 10 percent over the purchase price, reminding the committee that he had paid a 33 percent dealer's commission.[16] Smith, ignoring that it was he who had instigated the return of *Head,* was now implying that the museum was seeking a profit in its offer of a partial exchange. By now the museum found itself enmeshed in a controversy that could only create ill will for it. An important potential acquisition had degenerated into a petty squabble. In the end, the museum retained *Head* and Smith kept all of his "later and more important examples."[17]

Smith still resented the museum's behavior in its acquisition of *Head,* and his experience of its attempt to obtain a new work did nothing to mollify him. Barr's actions gave Smith the opportunity to expand an indiscretion into a cause célèbre and to cast himself as David to the museum's Goliath. If there was a loser in the contest, it was the museum, which had once again been shown to have taken an antagonistic stance in its dealings with an artist. Though well-meaning statements at the Woodstock conferences perennially gave the impression that artist and museum director had common interests, Smith graphically demonstrated that they also had great differences. While Smith had lost a sale that he could ill afford to lose, the Modern was also in an awkward position. Despite its reputation as the leading institution of contemporary art, it had no major work by the artist whom increasing numbers of artists and critics were recognizing as the most important American sculptor. By this time, in 1953, several major and some prestigious smaller institutions had acquired recent Smith works; the Modern was in the embarrassing position of being unable to obtain one directly from Smith. For the time being it compromised by purchasing a lesser work of recent vintage, *24 Greek Y's,* from a collector. Smith, deliberately or not, had forced the museum's hand: it could either ignore him and compromise its reputation or make amends. In 1957 the museum gave Smith a show that greatly gratified him, as evidenced by his gift of a *Medal for Dishonor* and a bronze relief, *Chicago Circle* (1956–57), to the museum in the name of his children.[18] It was a gift that "touched and delighted" Barr.[19]

After his return from Arkansas, a shortage of money—always a problem for Smith—necessitated his taking another teaching position. Henry Hope, chairman of the art department at Indiana University in Bloomington, had for several years been eager to have Smith visit the university. Previous efforts had failed, primarily because Smith asked for a salary higher than the department could pay. In fall 1954 its sculpture instructor, Robert Laurent, was leaving for a year's stay in Rome. The way was open to hire Smith for a ten-month period. Once again, however, his salary presented a problem. Smith had learned from George Rickey, a friend on the faculty, how much Laurent had been paid, and he expected to receive the same amount. Hope had intended to hold back on Smith's salary in order to supplement Laurent's stipend.[20] Eventually, however, he agreed to the full salary, and in addition gave Smith a month's leave to teach at the University of Mississippi.

In July 1954 Smith was commissioned to execute a stair rail and two sculptures by the collector who became his first patron, G. David Thompson, a Pittsburgh steel man. Because Smith considered that he alone was responsible for the arrangement with Thompson, he paid no commission to Willard. In December he raised the prices of all his works except those sold to Thompson. By mid-July 1955 he and Thompson had become quite friendly (Thompson sent baby gifts for the Smiths' daughter, Rebecca, born in April 1954, and for the new baby, Candida, due in August). At Thompson's suggestion, Smith sent him a list of materials he was seeking for projected stainless steel sculptures sixteen to twenty feet high. He was looking for off-sizes, he said, as warehouse stock was "too precise, polished and ground to .002 perfection."[21]

Smith's relationship with Thompson widened further his rift with Marian Willard. He was convinced now that he could do as well without her. He had already shown a strong antipathy toward commissions and museum discounts. A letter from Herman Cherry contains the implication that Smith had been complaining over the size of commissions being paid to Willard.[22] From 1954 on, Smith began unreasonably to question Willard's accounting methods, insisting that new arrangements would have to be made but never specifying the changes he wanted. He may have been attempting to justify his failure to pay commissions on the sales to G. David Thompson, though Willard had never asked for any.

In late 1955 Smith and Willard made plans for another one-man exhibition, his "biggest

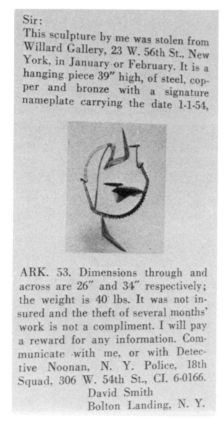

Sir:
This sculpture by me was stolen from Willard Gallery, 23 W. 56th St., New York, in January or February. It is a hanging piece 39" high, of steel, copper and bronze with a signature nameplate carrying the date 1-1-54,

ARK. 53. Dimensions through and across are 26" and 34" respectively; the weight is 40 lbs. It was not insured and the theft of several months' work is not a compliment. I will pay a reward for any information. Communicate with me, or with Detective Noonan, N. Y. Police, 18th Squad, 306 W. 54th St., CI. 6-0166.
David Smith
Bolton Landing, N. Y.

Fig. 33. David Smith letter to the editor, *Art News*, April 1956.
© ARTnews, 1956

and best.''[23] He seemed convinced that the success he had wanted for so long was now within his grasp. He wanted to show works made from 1953 through 1956. The "Forgings" series of 1955 was much on his mind and he wanted to show all "verticals." Smith was particularly concerned about advertising and volunteered to pay a part of its cost. "Ads, reviews, catalogs add to my standing but results do not pay off immediately but generally speaking it is cumulative I'm sure."[24] When the show was held, in March 1956, however, he was bitterly disappointed. Despite a personal expenditure of several hundred dollars in advertising and announcements, he sold nothing. At the end of the year he discovered that substantially less than half of his 1956 income was derived from the Willard Gallery. It was, he felt, a time for retreat and re-evaluation.[25] That re-evaluation was to leave no place for Marian Willard. The results of his March show apparently convinced him that it was time to sever connections. He required only a pretext, and one came.

Space in the Willard Gallery was at such a premium in 1955 that some of Smith's sculptures were stored in the basement. Neither Smith nor Willard was happy about the situation, and in September she asked him to pick up the stored works, including a hanging piece, *Ark 53*, which was in need of repair. He delayed. When finally the works were removed from the gallery, *Ark 53* was missing. Smith decided it had been stolen and wrote a letter to the editor of *Art News*, offering a reward for its return (Fig. 33). Overlooking the fact that he had ignored several requests to remove his sculptures from the basement, Smith condemned the gallery for failing to safeguard his works and withdrew its right to represent him. Marian Willard was convinced that the work had not been stolen; she suspected that when a new oil burner was installed and the old one discarded, *Ark 53* had been carted off with it.[26] Whatever the actual circumstances, it was perhaps more than coincidental that at the time of the controversy, both the Museum of Modern Art and the Corcoran Gallery in Washington offered to exhibit Smith's works the following year. With such bright prospects, Smith may have seen no need for the Willard Gallery. Herman Cherry wrote to Smith that at last "the mountain was coming to Mohammed."[27]

8

THE BEGINNING OF
A NEW ART

After 1950 Smith began to develop his work into something more than an inventive use of traditional ideas. He began to explore the notion of frontality, a concern that became a constant in an oeuvre noted for its eclecticism. The genesis of this concern lay in Smith's early reluctance to commit himself either to painting or to sculpture. Though he ultimately accepted the label of sculptor, Smith continued to maintain a painter's interest in the depiction of things as well as the sculptor's interest in the making of objects. And, unlike most sculptors, he had no interest in keeping painters' and sculptors' prerogatives separate. His ties with the New York painters enabled him to move freely among their ideas and adopt them for his own. By 1950 the painter's impulse became more evident. Smith introduced frames into his sculpture, first in *The Letter* (Fig. 27). Implicit in that device is the existence of a surface that could act as a picture plane and Smith began to use the surface that way in 1950.

Along with the picture plane Smith borrowed another, correlative idea of great importance to the New York painters, that of the vacant central area. A traditional composition comprises a central focal image with surrounding areas of lesser visual interest. When the image is removed from the center, however, the entire canvas essentially becomes the picture, and the viewer's eye is compelled to move over a considerable area rather than concentrate on a central focal point. An exchange of letters with Herman Cherry reveals Smith's awareness of parallels between painting and sculpture and his sense of the vacant center as an important sculptural device.

> Dec. 14–51
> 48 Cooper Square
> NY

Dear Dave; You seem to be under a miscomprehension about the c "bars" crossing the inactive center. You generalize and assume I don't consider it valid from your point of view. I do. In this case it assumes enormous importance for me aesthetically. All the activity, the curved and jagged shapes, are on the boundries [sic] leaving the center a vast emptiness not helped any by the flatness of the sculpture. . . .

> Cherry[1]

Dear Herman,

I've thought over the straight untouched bar—your objection is such I don't hold—but if the bar shape is obvious to you o.k.—when making it, it performed o.k. for me—why don't you object to the white of canvas as a technical space. . . . I've succeeded each year to make some denial of my past and leap out though this may not be evident to others—any bar I use is mine—bent or not as a tube color is yours. . . .

Regards,

David

Both Cherry and Smith seem to have been acknowledging that Smith was no longer concerned with the making of objects. Just as the New York painters were pulling away from a central image, so was Smith abandoning the monolithic object. With its denseness, the object becomes in its own way a center of focus. Though it lacks the "filler" areas that surround the central image of a painting, the object's density gives it stability, so that the eye seeks no further: all that needs to be seen is there at the focal area. By contrast, in speaking of Smith's work Cherry used such words as "activity," "jagged," and "curved." Indeed, so active are Smith's boundary areas that perhaps Cherry felt even more keenly the vacuum at the center. Though not yet so dramatically as later in his career, Smith had begun to deal with an art of spaces rather than one of volumes.

Smith first defined the area of the picture plane by framing its border. In variation, he also used frames to divide planes into subsections that became sculptures themselves, within the whole, as in *Hudson River Landscape* (Fig. 1), *The Banquet* (Fig. 34), and *Australia* (Fig. 32), all made in 1951. To the extent that Smith's frames delimit the space occupied by the work of art, they play much the same role as the frames used around paintings, with one difference: in Smith's sculptures the frames define the presence of the picture plane, a role that in painting is played by the canvas. Consequently, while a frame is often a decorative accessory to a painting, it is intrinsic to Smith's works, at least the early ones.

The picture plane was central to Smith's ideas after 1950. For him it was the matrix that linked and organized the parts. Eventually the frame was supplanted by baselines or by parts of the work skillfully oriented to imply the existence of a plane, though in the late "Cubi" pieces Smith returned to the use of frames in a slightly different context. A precedent for the use of planes as matrices exists in the "decks" of the "table-top tableaux" of the 1940s. Like the vertical planes, the horizontal decks define peripheries and organize the sculptures, as they are the one component that touches all other parts.

In view of Smith's interest in both painting and drawing, it is curious that he failed to arrive at frontality in sculpture through collage, as Picasso had in making his 1912 *Guitar*. *The Letter*, for example, seems even more closely related to collage in both subject and format than does the Picasso. Yet we have no evidence that Smith had any interest in collage, despite its uniqueness as an art form that combines both two- and three-dimensional elements. Instead, Smith saw painting and sculpture in terms of their physical properties,

Fig. 34 *The Banquet,* 1951. Steel. 53⅛ × 80¾ × 13½". Collection National Trust for Historic Preservation, Washington, D.C. Bequest of Nelson A. Rockefeller. Photo by Charles Uht, courtesy Rockefeller Collection

so that he could, as we saw earlier, comfortably compare thicknesses of Chinese carved sculptures with those of the paint of Van Gogh's and Cezanne's works.

The first sculptures deliberately based on the picture plane were made between 1950 and 1952. They were characterized by a return to the open linear constructions of the 1930s. Like Smith's earlier works, they were small sculptures intended to be displayed on non-sculptural supports so that they could be viewed at eye level. These are the works that Clement Greenberg, seeing the compression of linear components within vertical planes, described as "drawings in air." The titles of those works, including *24 Greek Y's, 17 h's, The Forest, 36 Bird Heads* (all of 1950), and *Four Soldiers* and *Hudson River Landscape* (both of 1951) testify to Smith's interest in the interaction among multiple images and to a move away from the constraints of the monolithic object. Though Smith made his "drawings in air" for only two years, he carried their sense of linearity through into his later work.

The Letter can for practical purposes be considered the first of the "drawings in air." Smith had found the letter forms that he used in this and several other works many years earlier in a hardware store in Glens Falls, New York.[2] *The Letter* was made after a lovers' quarrel with Jean Freas and was intended to speak for Smith in his attempt to bring her back.[3] The salutation reads "Dear Jeano," and the body of the letter is filled with sexual references. The *V* form, Smith's bisexual symbol, is modified into *Y*'s and the placement of "peckerhead" birds within *O* forms makes that letter's meaning quite clear. These are the "letter symbols" that Smith mentioned in his "letter of intentions" to the Guggenheim directors. Thus *The Letter* combines visual symbols with private verbal references.

With one exception, *Amusement Park* (1938), nothing in Smith's previous work anticipates the flat vertical structure of *The Letter*. Since the work was intended as a message to be read, Smith set it upright like a poster. He strengthened the impression of a written message by locating the letters on a vertical plane and restricting three-dimensional shapes—relics from the "table-top tableaux"—to the space behind them. Smith even simulated linear perspective with the exaggerated recession of the signature: it breaks out of the vertical plane, starting well in front and diminishing in size before coming to rest on the plane itself.

The function of *The Letter*'s forms as both symbols and letters is augmented by another function, as shapes with individual visual interest—a problematical one since they all are identical. In developing a solution to the problem, Smith introduced an important idea: a way of handling modular form. Individually the forms of *The Letter* could not compete visually with the complexities found in traditional monolithic forms, so the letter forms were left lying about in Smith's shop for quite some time before he was inspired with a way to use them. The *O* forms presented less of a problem than the *Y*'s, since they could act as frames for the various three-dimensional forms. To avoid tedious repetition, Smith placed the *Y*'s not only on the horizontal bars but partially below them and upside down as well. Though he would become increasingly inventive in the diverse ways in which he would use modular forms in the future, the principle of repetition and variation (one of his favorite phrases) had been established.

In *24 Greek Y's* (1950; Fig. 35) Smith distilled the theme of repetition and variation. The idea of a message is evident again in both title and image. Just as *The Letter* conveys an impression of English words, the *24 Greek Y's* seems to have associations with the Greek language, though of course neither work carries any actual verbal communication.[4] Where *Y* forms of *The Letter* are invested with the same sexual symbolism as Smith's earlier work, in *24 Greek Y's* they are not. Smith's use of private symbols steadily decreased after *The Letter,* and the visual associations that replaced them made his work much more comprehensible to the public. The *24 Greek Y's* has an austerity that is far removed from Smith's usual exuberance: he seems deliberately to have eliminated extraneous factors in order to focus on a specific problem. Indeed, the "drawings in air" of 1950 and 1951 are characterized in general by experimentation with one issue—the ways in which the picture plane might be used.

A comparison of the treatment of the picture plane in *The Letter* and in *24 Greek Y's* indicates that *The Letter* is the earlier work. In *The Letter,* the plane is a by-product of Smith's effort to simulate the two-dimensional page of a letter. The projecting signature is the only inventive element. The plane's parallel subdivisions are nothing more than simulations of the ruled lines of a page; its frame outlines the edges. At first glance the chief visual concern of *24 Greek Y's* seems to be either its modular *Y's* or the central axis. The viewer is not likely to think about an invisible plane. Its presence can only be inferred from the way in which the elements are aligned. Actually, however, there is little in this work that does not refer to that plane. Because it is only implied, evidence of its existence must come from the way other components are used—in this instance, the piling-up of forms in parallel planes and the action of the center axis.

One could argue that since the *Y's* are symbolic in *The Letter,* they may also be symbolic in *24 Greek Y's.* But two things argue against symbolism as their primary function. This piece lacks the supporting evidence of the bird-head forms and other cryptic three-dimensional objects that appear in *The Letter.* And the number of *Y's* and the deliberate regularity of their placement over a large surface manifest a concern with the modular form. Yet it is not the components themselves that interest us, for they are almost identical; the only irregularities involve the spaces that they enclose and that in turn surround them. Now the viewer could point to the central axis as an element of far greater importance than an invisible plane. Indeed, the axis commands attention as it swells and thins, and the randomly placed baselines also call attention to themselves with their irregular contours, two of them violating their purpose by arching gracefully upward from the horizontal. Yet the axis and its attendant baselines have flat, lifeless surfaces that become expressive only in silhouette. It is interesting to see that the photographer also took note of the silhouette's importance and placed *24 Greek Y's* in a position where it would cast a noticeable shadow.

The exchange of letters between Cherry and Smith, which had begun in December 1951, is relevant here. Smith evidently took exception to what he saw as Cherry's objection to "leaving the center a vast emptiness." Hence the question was raised as to why Cherry didn't also object to the white of the painter's canvas. Smith's response, though muddy, was clearly intended to draw a parallel between the emptiness in the center of his sculpture

Fig. 35. *24 Greek Y's,* 1950. Painted forged steel. 42¾ × 29⅛". Collection and photo courtesy The Museum of Modern Art, New York. Blanchette Rockefeller Fund

(*Hudson River Landscape*) and the use of white canvas as an active component in the paintings of the New York painters. (He could have easily been thinking of Franz Kline's work.) Smith's response showed his identification with the New York painters. Leaving the center vacant in this instance—and merely unfocused in others—enabled Smith to pull away from treating sculpture as an art of objects. Just as the New York painters were now beginning to concentrate on fields of color rather than forms within a field, so was Smith becoming more concerned with sculptural fields (still flatly vertical at this stage) that encompassed both forms and nonforms, that is to say, negative spaces.

In *The Banquet* (Fig. 34) Smith continued to exploit the picture plane by using the frame to emphasize its presence. The interlocked grid brought this work very close to the contemporaneous pictographs of Adolph Gottlieb. The Gottliebs had been close friends of Smith and Dorothy Dehner since their days at the Art Students' League, and it should not be surprising if Smith was influenced by the work of his painter friend. In *The Banquet* Smith explored a rather ingenious question: did his linear components constitute modules or act as frames to define spaces? Perhaps he had noted an important difference between the modules of *24 Greek Y's* and those of *17 h's* (1950; Fig. 36). All of the modules in *17 h's* perch squarely on baselines. Each *h* form completely encloses an area of space and thus doubles as a frame. In *24 Greek Y's*, the triangular areas are only incompletely enclosed by the modules surrounding them. The single exception is the *M* formed by two *Y*'s in the right middle section.

The ambiguity between module and frame is deepened in *The Banquet*. The dual nature of the fishlike forms at the top can be recognized at once. More subtle is the *h* module that forms one side of the uppermost horizontal frame. The far side of the *h* module does not rest on a horizontal support but remains suspended in exactly the same way as the inverted *Y*'s, establishing its kinship with the modular *Y*'s. Consider the difference if the foot of the *h* were to rest on the horizontal. It would be no longer a module but another frame; no ambiguity would result. On the bottom rung of the grid the *h* appears in the same position but this time with a truncated stem, whose missing member had been placed next to it. We cannot help comparing it with the *Y* module diagonally above it. Two arcs, cut from an *O* module, also appear in this sector, offering an additional variation.

The effect of line has probably never been more fully explored in sculpture than it is here. Its fundamental purpose seems to be to turn space into the most active component of the sculpture. The bars of the various frames take on life only in the way that they move through the picture plane. Otherwise they remain inert. Nowhere in the composition is the active quality of the space more noticeable than within the *O* forms. The activity of the space becomes more visible when we imagine a reversal of line and negative space. Earlier works indicate that Smith himself first perceived line and plane this way. In *Steel Drawing I* (Fig. 37) and *Steel Drawing II*, for example, both made in 1945, the picture planes are of solid steel, and the lines, cut by a torch, are only implied by the gaps where the metal was removed.

As in the other linear works, Smith used depth in *The Banquet* as well as line to create awareness of the picture plane. In *The Letter* he used a three-dimensional signature; in *24*

Fig. 36. *17 h's,* 1950. Painted steel. 43 × 28½ × ¾". Collection Candida and Rebecca Smith. Photo by David Smith

Fig. 37. *Steel Drawing I,* 1945. Steel. 22¼ × 26 × 6″. Collection and photo courtesy Hirshhorn Museum and Sculpture Garden, Smithsonian Institution, Washington, D.C.

Greek Y's a small circular disk was placed in the upper right sector. In *The Banquet*, gentle tipping of the *O* forms warns that depth still exists in the flattest of sculptures. Even the solid three-dimensional plates on the left, which may be intended to simulate fabric—a napkin or a tablecloth—remind us of the materiality of sculpture.

By the end of 1951 Smith had stopped focusing on the space of the picture plane. At least temporarily, the picture plane seemed to limit the scale on which he was determined to work. The change did not, however, mean the end to an art of spaces. Smith was first attracted to welding because of its capacity to permit forms to be swung into space, and he did not forget an idea that had so forcefully grasped him when it was new. Another idea had been gestating in the late 1940s and it came to fruition in 1951, enabling Smith simultaneously to use the picture plane and to incorporate the third dimension. The picture plane seemed rooted in Smith's painter inclinations; his second direction was rooted in object making. What evolved was a format based on the human figure in combination with a linear style. Though the human figure had been the traditional source for monolithic sculpture, what Smith had learned from working on the picture plane kept him from continuing in that conventional direction.

The human figure presented a problem to Smith's work. It did not lend itself to the flat, frontal style he had been developing. Indeed, the flowing, organic nature of the body is the reason for the use of mediums that may be modeled. Smith, however, saw in the figure a way to expand the scale on which he could work and spent the better part of the 1950s trying to reconcile the human form with the flatness characteristic of welded metals. Though he eventually found ways to use his open, linear style of 1950 and 1951 on a large scale without reference to the figure, anthropomorphism usually remained a part of Smith's work, despite the attendant awkwardness.

The first full-scale sculptures on which Smith worked were those in the "Tanktotem" series, all of which are anthropomorphic (see *Tanktotem I*, 1952, Fig. 38; *V*, 1955–56, Fig. 39). The picture plane is maintained in the figures' torsos, from which modular forms sprout in simulation of anatomical parts. By Smith's count, there were ten "Tanktotems," the first made in 1952 and the last in 1960. All were designed around tank or drum lids, usually cleverly altered. It can be presumed that the idea of recasting those industrial objects for art purposes came from the *Y's*, *h's*, and other modules of the "drawings in air." In the "Tanktotems," Smith discovered an alternative to bases: he devised a tripod arrangement that eliminated the plinth necessary to more traditionally sculpted figures. Occasionally the third leg was even outfitted with an anthropomorphic foot.

Although Smith did not begin to number and name his works in series until 1952, beginning with the "Tanktotems" and "Agricolas," *The Hero* (Fig. 40) of 1951 properly belongs with the "Tanktotems." It contains nearly all of the characteristics of that first large-scale series. If we include *The Hero* in that group, however, *Canopic Head*, also of 1951 (Fig. 41), would have to be considered the immediate precursor of the "Tanktotems"—and clearly it is in quite another vein.

Despite the expressive linearity that relates it to the "drawings in air," the dominant characteristics of *Canopic Head* are the same as those of the anthropomorphic works that

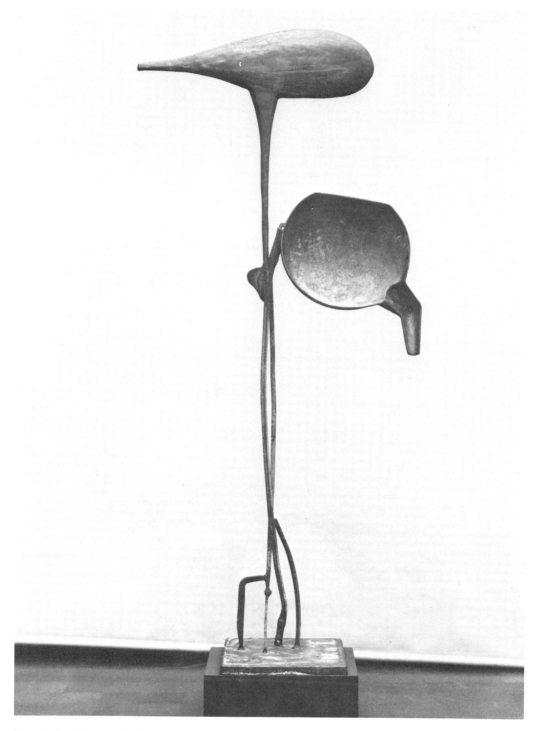

Fig. 38. *Tanktotem I (Tanktotem Pouring)*, 1952. Steel. 90 × 39″. Collection and photo courtesy The Art Institute of Chicago. Gift of Mr. and Mrs. Jay Z. Steinberg

Fig. 39. *Tanktotem V,* 1955–56. Steel. 96¾ × 51 × 15″. Collection and photo courtesy Howard and Jean Lipman, Cannondale, Connecticut. Photo by Rudolph Burckhardt

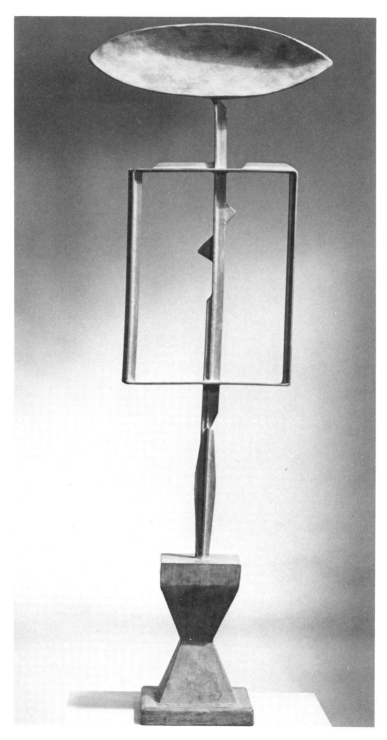

Fig. 40. *The Hero*, 1951. Painted steel. 73¹¹⁄₁₆ × 25½ × 11¾″. Collection and photo courtesy Brooklyn Museum, New York. Dick S. Ramsay Fund

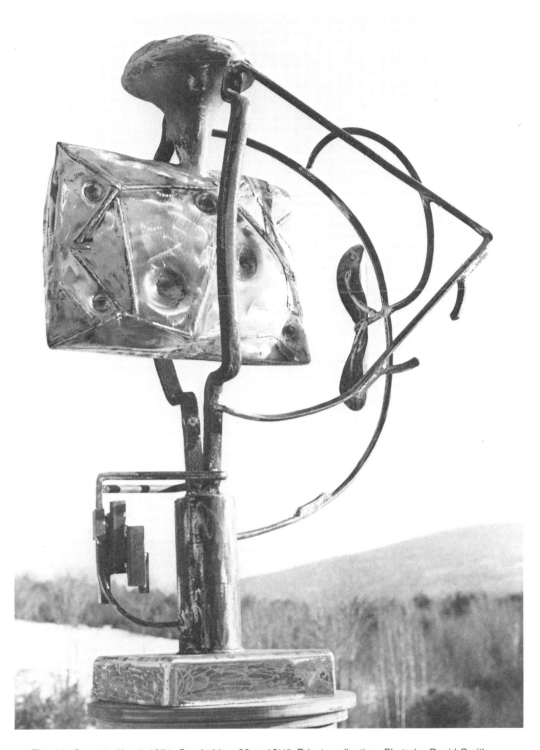

Fig. 41. *Canopic Head,* 1951. Steel. 44 × 33 × 18½″. Private collection. Photo by David Smith

were soon to follow. The combination of head, torso, and heavy base sets the pattern that is repeated in *The Hero*. It is interesting to note that *Canopic Head* actually combines two torsos at right angles to each other, one solid and the other linear, thus bringing together the solid frontal torsos of later "Tanktotems" and the open-framed torso of *The Hero*. The upper part of the head is actually a horizontal tank end that has been distorted, along with the torso, and then welded onto a necklike form. The same sort of head-and-neck arrangement is also found in *Egyptian Landscape* of 1951 (Fig. 18), but turned on its side to function as a phallus shape. Further comparison of *Canopic Head* and *Egyptian Landscape* reveals that these two works, despite their shared symbols, linearity, and themes based on ancient Egypt, demonstrate the two different directions in which Smith was working. *Egyptian Landscape*, like most of Smith's horizontal constructions, has a pictorial quality that faded when Smith began working in a vertical format. Whether or not Smith found in the horizontal format a special impetus for exploring space, the fact remains that his anthropomorphic (and vertical) sculptures are less successful in embracing space.

The first three "Tanktotems" (I include *The Hero* as one) are particularly revealing as transitional works: they contain important characteristics of the small-scale symbolic works of the 1940s side by side with those of Smith's late, major works. Rosalind Krauss points out that *Cubetotem 7 and 6* (1961) ought to be included among the "Tanktotems." She sees it as a "conceptual bridge" to the "Cubi" series of the 1960s, sometimes considered to be Smith's most important body of work.[5] The "Tanktotem" series may be thought of as the chief link between the 1940s and the late work. The ten numbered works span the years 1952 through 1960; it is a considerable length of time for the creation of so few works but indicates Smith's tendency to work and rework an image.

The early "Tanktotems" are related to the fierce primitive forms of Gonzalez and even more closely to those of Lipchitz. Smith had kept a watchful eye on Lipchitz, whose work, illustrated in a 1935 edition of *Cahiers d'art*, catalyzed ideas for sculpture at that time. Smith had also visited Lipchitz's studio in Paris during the Smiths' trip to Europe in 1935 and 1936.[6] By 1942 Smith regarded Lipchitz as a competitor; after meeting him at a party given by Marian Willard, Smith wrote her, "I can feel a stimulating sense of rivalry."[7] The early 1950s saw the advent of Smith's totemic structures, whose singular demonic themes replaced those of the episodic tabletop "Spectres" of the 1940s and moved him closer in spirit to Lipchitz's work.

The similarity of theme and treatment in Smith's and Lipchitz's work can be seen clearly by a comparison of *The Hero* and Lipchitz's *Figure* (1926–30; Fig. 42). Most immediately noticeable is the surrealistic effect of the concave heads common to both. Smith formed *The Hero's* head by removing the center portion of a tank lid and then welding the outer pieces together. Other similarities appear in the strongly linear torsos and massive bases. Even the positioning of *Canopic Head's* two frontal planes, one at right angles to the other, may have been derived from a similar juxtaposition in Lipchitz's *Figure*. In all, it is difficult to escape the conclusion that the first full-scale sculpture of Smith's late period was much influenced, if not precipitated, by the Lipchitz work.

There are, of course, important differences between Lipchitz's and Smith's work, and

Fig. 42. Jacques Lipchitz. *Figure,* 1926–30. Bronze (cast 1937). 85¼ × 38⅝". Collection and photo courtesy The Museum of Modern Art, New York. Van Gogh Purchase Fund

they too may be seen in *The Hero* and *Figure*. Some differences are attributable to the techniques the two artists used—casting for Lipchitz, welding for Smith—but the essential differences are those of attitude. Despite its linearity, Lipchitz's *Figure* is primarily sculpture in the round and similar in feeling to his cagelike structures of the 1930s. The frontality of the head is negated by the four-sided composition of the torso and the rounded base. The abstract torso has been woven into a carefully worked decorative design that is consistent with its carefully textured surface. Lipchitz remained comfortably within the traditions of bronze sculpture, his menacing form tempered by the flawless construction that is characteristic of professional foundries.

The Hero, in contrast, displays a harshness not only in the treatment of its theme but in the material and its processing. The traditional sense of form and balance is upset by an overweighted base (Smith had not yet thought of using a tripod) that leaves the linear center section almost disembodied. *The Hero* is divided into three distinct sections, only minimally integrated. The welded connections remain evident and uneven (in contrast to the uniformly textured skin of Lipchitz's *Figure*) so that the work has a fabricated appearance more usually associated with the factory than the studio. Smith covered the surface with red lead—a practical step if the sculpture were to remain out of doors (as it did, since the proliferation of his sculpture had made storage a serious problem), but one totally unrelated to the requirements of the forms. Essentially, then, *The Hero* is discontinuous in its parts, unlike the smooth-flowing surface of *Figure* which unifies the various segments. This difference is heightened by the mediums the two sculptors used. Lipchitz's bronze had been poured as a single form, whereas the welded sections of *The Hero* were added one after another. Thus *The Hero*'s lack of the monolithic quality so noticeable in *Figure* is as much a by-product of the method of fabrication as it is the result of Smith's opposition to the idea of monolithism.

One aspect of *The Hero* is quite curious. This work is autobiographical, as Smith said all of his works were.[8] At six feet, two inches, its height approximated Smith's own of six feet, one inch, and the hard coarse forms corroborate Smith's self-image. Yet mounted on the central shaft are two triangular forms that can be interpreted only as breasts. They are derived from the claw symbol that Smith associated with women (a device also used by Giacometti). Its use here leads to interesting speculations. Did Smith have doubts about his own masculinity? Did he perceive the grasping qualities he associated with claws and women to be a part of his own nature? The forms had to be carefully cut out, welded onto the shaft, and then ground down until they were well integrated with the structure. A sculptor would have to be strongly disposed to self-revelation in order to carry through the necessary technical processes.

Though the first "Tanktotems" appear to be radically different from the tableaux of the 1940s, they still use the same symbolism. The upper section of *The Hero* may seem only marginally related to the "peckerhead," but in *Tanktotem I* (Fig. 38) we find this symbol in its most graphic form, divested of any secondary meanings or artistic trappings. The way in which Smith fashioned his forms made it clear that the next logical direction for the "peckerhead" would be a simple head-and-neck arrangement, such as we see in *Sitting*

Fig. 43. *Sitting Printer,* 1954. Bronze. 87¼ × 15¾ × 16″. Collection and photo courtesy Storm King Art Center, Mountainville, New York

Fig. 44. *Portrait of a Painter,* 1954. Bronze. 96⅜ × 24½ × 11⅞″. Collection Candida and Rebecca Smith. Photo courtesy Marlborough Gallery, New York

114

Fig. 45. *Portrait of a Lady Painter,* 1957. Bronze. 63⅝ × 59¾ × 12½″. Collection and photo courtesy Storm King Art Center, Mountainville, New York

Printer (1954; Fig. 43). With *Tanktotem I* Smith seems to have exhausted his use of this particular symbol, and in *Tanktotem II, III,* and *IV* he retreated to the insectile format of the mid-1930s.

Since the start of his career Smith had invariably begun his sculptures with a specific idea in mind, seeking the most efficient means and materials to carry it out. In concentrating on totemic imagery during the making of the early "Tanktotems," he often overlooked the creative possibilities of the welding process which might have suggested themselves. Then in 1955 the suggestion was made which broke the pattern of rigid adherence to anatomical order and which refocused Smith on the evolving process of making sculpture. Clement Greenberg has written:

> Sometime close to or in 1955 Helen Frankenthaler and I visited Smith in Bolton Landing. There was a Tanktotem he was working on to the right of the road in front of his shop. He hadn't yet put his usual drum-head on top of it, and I said why not leave it off, leave it decapitated, and if necessary stick it in at the hips or add it there. "Tanktotem V" was the result. Of which I'm proud. I like to think, out of vanity, that my suggestion made itself felt in other works, but wdn't claim it.[9]

Tanktotem V (Fig. 39) shows how radically the anthropomorphic image was altered by the transplanting of its head. With that change, the work calls to mind the descriptiveness of the "drawings in air." Forms exist gracefully in space, and the rigid spine that in earlier anthropomorphic works had plunged down the central axis has now been moved to a less conspicuous position at the side. No comparison better illustrates Smith's experimentation with the positions of head and neck than that of the vertical *Portrait of a Painter* (1954; Fig. 44) with the horizontal *Portrait of a Lady Painter* (1957; Fig. 45).

9

WORKING METHODS, 1953–57

Smith placed his first order with Ryerson Steel Fabricators in August 1951. During 1961 his orders for stainless steel from that company alone totaled over three and a half tons.[1] In the same year a partial list of sales totaled over $81,000. By 1963 pieces in the "Cubi" series were being priced, and sold, at over $50,000 each, and large sculptures were being shipped regularly to Europe for exhibition. Though small by the standards of industry, for art this was big business. Yet fifteen years earlier, Smith had been hailed by W. R. Valentiner as the modern successor to early American folk artists and craftsmen. In a plea for a return to uniquely American art, Valentiner had deplored both European influences and the love of machinery which was "far in advance of a spiritual development in the arts."[2] With a successful factory crammed with modern machinery and several workmen on his payroll, had Smith succumbed to mammon? Had he sacrificed his earlier pride in craftsmanship for the manufacture of soulless, machinelike sculptures, or had some fusion finally taken place between the "spiritual" and the "Machine Age" forms? In 1952 a way to mesh European influence and machine techniques was very clear to Smith, if not to Valentiner:

> American machine techniques and European cubist tradition both of this century are accountable for the new freedom in sculpture making. Sculpture is no longer limited to slow carving of marble and long process of bronze. Here I am talking about direct metal construction, contrary to the carving away technique of classical sculpture, the new method is assemble the whole by adding its unit parts . . . is also an industrial concept, the basis of automobile and machine assembly in the steel process.[3]

Two things had occurred during 1950. The first, already discussed, was Smith's work with the picture plane; the other was his return to the almost exclusive use of welded steel. Smith's genius lay in his ability to synthesize material and technique with the forms they were used to make. So complete a synthesis had not been achieved in sculpture since the invention of wood and stone carving. We are indebted to Smith for the wide acceptance that welding now enjoys as a legitimate technique for making art; such acceptance came because he created a sculptural vocabulary emancipated from the figure and intrinsic to the new medium.

Because the casting of bronze and the carving of stone have been the principal means of making sculpture for thousands of years, we have a tendency to overlook how closely wedded both techniques are to the monolithic form. The properties of molten metal are important in determining the type of form that can be made by the casting process. The large mass and limited surface area of a monolithic form are ideal for casting, since the metal remains liquid long enough to reach all parts of the mold. When a form is attenuated, as are the "drawings in air," for example, the molten metal is likely to solidify in a narrow passage, so that the rest of the mold remains unfilled. The monolithic form is suited also to carving stone, which is capable of bearing enormous loads but whose tensile strength is quite limited. Mute evidence of this weakness is found in the missing limbs and other salient features of so much of the statuary that survives from antiquity. These two techniques thus admirably support our narcissistic impulse to create images of ourselves (so long as we resist the temptation to fling our arms about) by providing the necessary vehicles to accommodate their mass. Indeed, the most "sculptural" of forms is considered the mass of the torso.

Smith's development as an artist was hindered for many years by the fact that his—and everyone's ideas about sculpture were based on the demands of the monolithic form. The word "sculpture" itself is derived from the Latin *sculptura*, from *scalpere*, to carve. Smith's post-1950 works show no trace of the bulk of carved works, but still we call them "sculptures." Smith's problem was that, like almost all American sculptors, except Ibram Lassaw, he had derived his knowledge of sculpture from monolithic sources, but was using a technique, welding, that was not then suitable for the production of that kind of art. Smith slowly became aware after many years that he would have to give up some of his cherished ideas about the nature of sculpture. To realize the potential of his medium, he would have to explore directions suggested by a work while he was making it. The use of preliminary sketches was harmful in this respect, because his preconceived ideas were influenced by the constraints of monolithic form.

Smith usually made sketches before he began a sculpture. Between 1936 and the early 1950s he filled well over forty sketchbooks with his ideas, most of them related to sculpture. Many of his drawings, with their figures modeled in lights and darks, suggest the influence of monolithic form, though the emphasis was always linear. Smith worked an idea over and over until he achieved an image that satisfied him. Only then, ordinarily, did he commit it to sculpture. The sketches were quite specific and called for complex sculptural techniques. Like blueprints they were intended to be carefully followed. Smith was enamored of the word "concept," which he saw as the idea brought into existence *prior* to the making of the sculpture. Before 1950 there was little or no emphasis on opportunities for improvisation which might arise during the sculpture-making process. In this respect, Smith was constricted by the methods of sculptors whose work was cast in bronze. Obviously such artists, who shipped their waxes to professional foundries, would fail to appreciate creative thinking by foundry workmen during the casting process.

His careful planning and preparation left him very little room to explore creative possibilities after a sculpture was begun. In an interview with Smith published in the September 1951 issue of *Art News,* Elaine de Kooning described in considerable detail the techniques Smith was using to make *Cathedral.* She noted that he usually started with drawings, though he had not done so in this instance. Even so, de Kooning wrote, "there always are weeks of preparation." Since *Cathedral* was to be related to church architecture, a group of bars had to be forged at right angles. For an "altar body," the limbs were first forged and then welded. The knob for a "twisted neck" was built up of welded steel. A micrometer was used to measure certain lengths, and a cutting torch was taken to a "shroud figure"; on the "talons" Smith used silver solder. He had so precisely defined his subject that it was not possible for him to use welding exclusively. The images determined the method. In other sculptures where even greater specificity was necessary, Smith cast his forms in bronze.[4]

The article was originally intended to showcase Smith's considerable technical skills to help him impress the Guggenheim directors enough that they would grant him a second fellowship. As in the past, Smith still lacked enough confidence in his art to permit it to stand alone; instead, he sought to impress by the skill he brought to a large number of complex and time-consuming techniques. In the end, the interview was published too late to influence the directors, but as we have seen, Smith received his grant anyway.

Smith told Elaine de Kooning that he had "no set procedure" in beginning a sculpture. Two years later, in Portland, Oregon, he could say, "I rarely work with a preconceived conviction about the end of the sculpture. I rarely work from a drawing."[5] These two statements reflect the important change that had taken place. The earlier one indicated flexibility only in the procedure; the latter extended flexibility to the planning stage as well. He had at last recognized that more could be learned from improvisation than by attempts to anticipate possibilities on a sheet of paper. Between 1936 and the early 1950s Smith filled over forty sketchbooks, only three between 1954 and 1957; after that, one. Though Smith still occasionally made sketches before beginning a sculpture, usually he did not. By the mid 1950s, drawing and sculpture had been separated as art forms.

When the drawings were freed from their function as a means to an end, they became independent works of art. Smith produced three to four hundred large drawings each year, on the finest paper; many he framed. As we can see in Figure 46, they are abstractions in flat rhythmic brushstrokes and contain no sense of modeled form. The drawings were executed with a speed and intensity that were characteristic of the works of the New York painters as well. Smith began to call on psychic forces within him, using the speed and fluency of his brush as a catalyst. Speaking at Tulane University in 1955, Smith said that the artist's "true personality" is often revealed in his drawings "before his own natural defenses can come to his defense." Drawing reveals the artist's "truth" better than other media with technique and tradition. Earlier he had said that "drawing is the most direct, closest to the true self."[6]

Still another influence was evidenced in the drawings of the early 1950s, when Jean Freas gave Smith a book on oriental painting, *The Spirit of the Brush.* From then on, Smith's writings and speeches often made reference to the brushwork of the Japanese and Chinese. Indeed, many of his drawings began to take on the look of oriental calligraphy.

Fig 46. Untitled drawing, 1958. Black egg ink. 22 × 30½″. Collection Candida and Rebecca Smith. Photo courtesy M. Knoedler & Co., Inc., New York

Calligraphic shapes were worked on the painted surfaces of some late sculptures and in the strokes made by the disc sander as Smith ground the surfaces of the cubes in his stainless-steel sculptures of the late 1950s and 1960s. An interesting combination of sculpture and calligraphic form may be seen in *Australian Letter* (1953; Fig. 47). Smith had made drawings on metal surfaces at least as early as 1946, when he corresponded with the Eastman Kodak Company in Rochester, New York, regarding the possibility of sensitizing metal surfaces with a film called "Transfax," used to place working drawings on flat metal surfaces.[7] A drawing in black ink was put in contact with sensitized metal and exposed to arc or mercury-vapor lights until the image transferred itself to the metal.

Smith continued to experiment periodically with ways of anticipating sculptures. One, developed in the late 1950s, involved the use of bits of cardboard cut to the proportions of his modular cubes. The pieces of cardboard were then affixed to sheets of paper and spray-painted, leaving stenciled images to be used in the construction of a sculpture. Smith called them "think pieces" (Fig. 48).[8]

When Smith had finally separated the art of sculpture from that of drawing he was free to explore the creative potential of welding. The features of welding differ radically from those of casting and carving. We should therefore not be surprised to find that the art based on those features differs in appearance as well. Welding is not merely an additive process, as is hand building in clay, for example, but a joining process. From the inception of the work the process presumes the existence of two parts to be joined. Because the parts are preformed, they are joined symbiotically rather than fused into a mass. The forms are recognizable both individually and as segments of the whole. Tension usually results as the viewer strives to integrate them.

The expressiveness of the sculptural space in this kind of art is vastly more important than the characteristics of the individual forms. There is no need to presume that the torch must also be used to construct forms; quite the contrary. Forming through welding is limited to the most simple geometrics. Random contouring leaves gaps to be plugged, welding beads are difficult to remove from joints, heat warps the steel, and its properties are too hard for all but the most limited type of forging. We can readily see why found objects are admirably suited to welded sculpture. (Found objects need not be literally found, of course; they need only possess no aesthetic qualities apart from those they acquire by their use in sculpture.) Because welding is an art of spaces, the forms themselves are of less importance and so the use of parts from sources far removed from art is completely acceptable. Though common enough today, this idea was new in the early 1950s and helped end the domination of curvilinear forms in sculpture.[9] Though Smith was not the first to be concerned with an art of spaces—he had been preceded by Picasso, the Constructivists, and at times Jacques Lipchitz, among others[10]—it was the variety of ways and the scale on which he worked that brought this type of art to widespread attention.

The use of found objects demands improvisation. Sketches cannot anticipate that point of stasis between the centrifugal tugging of individual parts and the artist's efforts to achieve the compensatory centripetal pull that enables him to achieve the optimum balance of forces. The interactions are so many and so various that only spontaneous work methods can succeed, as Smith finally recognized.

Fig. 47. *Australian Letter,* 1953. Painted steel. 79¾ × 107 × 16¾″. Private collection, Switzerland. Photo by Stanley E. Marcus

122

Fig. 48. Untitled drawing, 1961. Spray paint on paper. 17½ × 11⁷⁄₁₆″. Collection Candida and Rebecca Smith. Photo courtesy M. Knoedler & Co., Inc., New York

The "drawings in air" are transitional works; Smith was not yet able to free his work from certain elements that blocked his working in series as he did in his mature period. The "drawings in air," such as *Hudson River Landscape, Banquet,* and *The Letter,* depend, as their titles indicate, on sources besides the sculpture itself for their subjects. To some degree the choice of subject determined what the sculpture would look like, regardless of how abstract the work was. As mentioned earlier, the "Tanktotems" were highly anthropomorphic until Clement Greenberg suggested that Smith "decapitate" *Tanktotem V.* Once he could divorce the subject of a sculpture from outside referents, Smith was able to develop series, building from one work to another. Just as in the case of the *Y* forms, when the very presence of a found form suggested ideas, earlier works in a series catalyzed progressively more creative solutions for later ones. The effect is particularly evident in the "Voltri" and "Cubi" series.

The use of steel forms in the preparatory stages proved far more practical than sketches. Here frontality had an advantage over monolithic form. By laying the form on a flat surface and shuffling the parts until the arrangement was satisfactory, Smith knew precisely how the frontal plane would look before the pieces were permanently joined. Smith described the procedure which is illustrated in Figure 49: "Some works start out as chalk drawings on the cement floor, with cut steel forms working into the drawings. When it reaches the stage that the structure can become united, it is welded into position upright. Then the added dimension requires different considerations over the more or less profile form of the floor drawing assembly."[11] Smith enhanced the effectiveness of contrast by the use of whiting. Unlike the traditional process of working up from a base, laying out the forms enabled Smith greatly to increase his scale and work faster while maintaining a flat, frontal format. Because bars and plates of steel stock are customarily flat, the material itself also reinforced the use of a picture plane.

At this point Smith had to experiment. No technique was ever better suited to experimentation than welding, in which forms are joined instantaneously, so that they can be seen exactly as they will be in the final sculpture. Gone are the many stages of bronze casting, the need to imagine how wax images will look in bronze, and the tedious hours of stone carving. Massive forms can be supported as if they hung in space. Smith needed help, however, if he was to investigate the full possibilities of his medium. Inventory, storage, handling, a fire-proof work area, shipping—these were only some of the factors that had to be considered. Smith found ways of dealing with these aspects of his art not in the ateliers of sculptors, but in small factories that must have reminded him of the Midwest of his childhood.

In 1946 Smith began to purchase his materials from a fabricator, and Albany Steel Iron Company. During the 1950s he purchased tank lids, channel beams, and quantities of unassorted shapes left after fabricators had cut forms for other customers. For his second Guggenheim fellowship Smith committed himself to making eighteen sculptures. He actually produced twenty-two. In the following year he produced twenty-three. In 1953 he made a record thirty-three sculptures, including some very large ones. Storage of both sculptures and raw materials became an enormous problem.

Fig. 49. Work layout for shop, c. 1962. Photo by David Smith

Storage space at the Willard Gallery had been taxed by Smith's high rate of production as early as 1947. Sculptures were shipped to Bolton Landing or stored with friends like Herman Cherry. Late in 1950, when the Museum of Modern Art returned *Cello Player*, Marian Willard implored Smith to remove it to Bolton Landing, as the gallery was over-flowing. In 1953 Smith wrote in despair to Clement Greenberg that even though he had no money, he would somehow manage to pay for storage space if Greenberg could find any in New York.[12] Long before Smith's break with Willard over the alleged theft of *Ark 53*, the gallery had become unable to handle the number of sculptures coming from Smith's workshop. The only feasible place left for storage was the fields of Bolton Landing. Outdoor conditions in that harsh climate necessitated Smith's investigating various protective waxes to prevent his mild steel from rusting. The need for weather protection eventually became a major factor in his decision to paint his sculptures.

Storage of materials was also a problem. The odd shapes accumulated from fabricators were dumped outside the shop, near his entrance to the county road. Eventually he built a large deck on which he could pile the assortment of stainless-steel plates and cubes which he bought from Ryerson Steel and other fabricators. Those were the obvious materials that Smith required; in addition he needed myriad small items to keep the work flowing. Smith listed some of them:

> Stocks of bolts, nuts, taps, dies, paints, solvents, acids, protective coatings, oils, grinding wheels, polishing discs, dry pigments, waxes, chemicals, spare machine parts are kept stocked on steel shelving more or less patterned after a factory stock-room.
> Sheets of stainless steel, bronze, copper, aluminum are stocked in $\frac{1}{8}$'' $\times$ 4' $\times$ 8' for fabricating, cold and hot rolled 4' $\times$ 8' sheets are stocked outside the shop in thicknesses from 1'8'' to $\frac{7}{8}$''. Lengths of strips, shapes and bar stock are racked in the basement of the house or interlaced in the joists of the roof.[13]

Smith's workshop underwent several expansions after the first cinder-block building was erected in 1937. In its final form, in the early 1960s, the shop consisted of two rooms, each about forty feet long. The north side of its transite roof, twenty-five feet high at its peak, was pierced by a row of skylights. Space heaters at either end permitted Smith to work in the shop throughout the winter. A chain hoist had been set up in one room, and there Smith did his assembling and welding; the other room was used for the storage of supplies. Light came from three banks of fluorescent lights and a large garage door that was left open on warm days. As he could afford them, Smith acquired an arc welder, a heliarc welder (for stainless steel), oxyacetylene equipment, two automatic burning machines (to cut large circles), two electric chain hoists, a large air compressor, two cut-off machines (to cut bar stock), a drill press, an Acorn platen (a heavy-duty steel table of lattice construction capable of holding forms in awkward positions), two new burning tables, and hand tools.[14]

A persistent problem was obtaining sufficient electricity. The original shop had been built next to the road in order to avoid the high cost of running power lines to Smith's house. The operation of the arc welder on the local line installed by the Rural Electrification Administration in Depression years created disturbances and caused voltage to drop in neighboring houses; as a result, for many years Smith had to use a gasoline engine to drive his welder. It was, however, costly to run and generated uneven flows of current. Smith investigated the use of three-phase power, which produced a flow of current even steadier than the single-phase power locally available. A letter from Niagara Mohawk in March 1963 informed him that the charge would be $3,600.15.[15] Smith had the power line installed.

Though assembling work on the floor permitted him to greatly increase the scale, Smith was faced with the problem of raising the forms into the vertical position and welding the additional pieces that would enable a sculpture to stand. Just the moving of heavy steel forms was difficult for one person and in the late 1940s, Smith hired Leon Pratt, a local man who was handy with tools, to help him, first part-time and eventually full-time. In later years Pratt did almost all of the welding and was responsible for making the sculptures after Smith had arranged the parts. Despite a statement in 1964 that he employed no workmen,[16] Smith's 1963 payroll totaled $10,000 for three men, an amount of some concern to him.

The availability of men and machines to help him affected the appearance of Smith's work. Frontal sculptures, which comprised the bulk of the large-scale works, were not difficult—Smith could move pieces around in the floor layouts he had devised—but when he became interested in depth during the 1960s, he had problems. He and Pratt held forms of the "Cubi" series on precariously perched boxes until they found an acceptable arrangement. The method was limiting, cumbersome, and physcially exhausting. The purchase of an electric chain hoist eliminated the need to hold the forms manually. The hoist could dangle a form until Smith was satisfied with its position and had tack-welded it in place.[17] As the joining was only temporary, he could easily make changes later if he wanted to. Many of the early "Cubi" pieces are set on the floor; later works start from pedestals. Without the chain hoist, even two people would have had difficulty hoisting heavy steel forms to the top of a pedestal before developing the sculptural arrangement. Earlier "Cubi" sculptures consist of comparatively small cubes stacked conservatively one on another. As the series progressed, larger forms could be swung boldly into space. With the addition of two or three hoists, several large cubes could be arranged at one time.

The shipping of Smith's sculptures was also problematic. Heavy sculptures are expensive to ship by common carrier, and for many years Smith transported his own works in his pickup truck. Welded sculptures do not, of course, present the same problems as more delicate art objects. Yet for a time Smith's sculptures sustained a surprising amount of damage in transit. As noted earlier, in October 1956 he rejected an invitation to show his work in the upcoming Whitney Annual, an event in which he had always participated, because he was angry at the way his work had been crated after the last exhibition and the damage that had happened to it in transit.[18] A claim against Railway Express dragged on for months. Some of the many claims Smith made for damages are attributable to the enormous amount of exhibiting he did and others to his own fractious nature. Another factor, however, was that many of the found objects incorporated in the sculptures were of cast steel. It is extremely difficult to weld cast forms together successfully, a fact that Smith must have discovered the first time he tried it. Such a joint is brittle. At any noticeable jarring the parts separate. There is no evidence that Smith ever warned museums or galleries of this possibility, and people probably assumed that the works were more durable than in fact they were. When *Head* was knocked down in the Museum of Modern Art's sculpture garden in 1944, the welds shattered where they joined cast forms; had the forms not been cast, the sculpture would at worst have been only dented.

During his year at Indiana University, 1954–55, Smith learned a considerable amount about forging. Seward & Company, a Bloomington steel fabricator, employed a blacksmith named Leroy Borton. Smith would take his students to the shop and have Borton demonstrate his techniques. It was there, on Seward's power forge, that the "Forgings" series (Fig. 50) was made in 1955. As on other such occasions, Smith paid tribute to the knowledge, skill, and friendliness of the master craftsman by naming a work, *History of Leroy Borton,* for him.

Once Smith focused on welding as his main technique, his art making became quite costly. Smith claimed that during 1950 and 1951 he made only one sale, for $333. Whether or not the statement is strictly true, Smith obviously could not support himself on the sales of his art alone.[19] With the loss of Dorothy's small income his chief means of support was gone. In some bitterness he wrote to *Art News* on November 15, 1953, that at no time did returns meet the cost of production. "I have to earn by other means the right to produce my work." Those "means" were his teaching jobs.

The need for funds to operate his shop pressed heavily on Smith. By the mid-1950s he was operating on a scale that was unprecedented for him. Industrial techniques enabled him to increase his output but also created the problems faced by any small factory that does not sell enough of its product: salaries had to be met, bills paid, storage space located. In a letter to Marian Willard in 1950, Smith estimated his costs at five hundred dollars per piece and decided to raise his prices 20 percent.[20] In 1954 he raised them 25 percent and eliminated museum discounts.[21] Three months later he again raised his prices.[22]

Given his needs and aspirations, the price hikes were not unrealistic. For one thing, Smith understood the importance of exposure in creating demand for his work and was prepared to spend some of his limited funds on advertising (he had written to Willard in 1947: "Reproduction seems to sell work. . . . Reproduction seems to act as first acquaintance and eliminate some of the barriers").[23] Moreover, Smith had for many years hoped to use stainless steel. Now, in the mid-fifties, he was more determined to than ever. But it would be a costly undertaking (a statement of 1957 indicates expenses for shop operation and materials alone at almost $7,500).[24] If Smith was to reach his goal he had to command better prices. In October 1957 Dan Johnson, Marian Willard's husband, wrote to Lloyd Goodrich, then director of the Whitney, that a chief reason for Smith's separation from the Willard was the high prices Smith was asking. Johnson seemed to believe that Smith was being unreasonable.[25] The Whitney, however, had been interested in acquiring a sculpture, and Smith's Museum of Modern Art exhibition had closed only a few days before. He was on the verge of being able to afford to make sculpture the way he wanted to.

Fig. 50. "Forgings" series, 1955. Photo by David Smith

10

"SUCCESS
D' CASHINE"

In the 1950s the Museum of Modern Art inaugurated a series of exhibitions of "artists in mid-career," intended to emphasize "new talent."[1] One of the first artists selected was David Smith. According to Andrew Ritchie, then director of the Department of Painting and Sculpture, he was "the major American sculptor of our time although he had not yet received as much success as he deserved."[2] After thirty years in art, twenty of them as a sculptor, Smith hardly qualified as a "new talent." But he was still not widely known, and the prestige of a Modern exhibition might prove decisive in moving him at last out of the ranks of artists who were still labeled "new talent" or in "mid-career." Some such significant event, one that could focus on the accumulation of ideas incorporated in his work of the 1950s, seemed necessary if Smith was to become better known.

The museum had originally intended to confine its showings to recent works and to call the exhibitions "Works in Progress." The title was changed to "Artists in Mid-career" so that artists could show earlier works as well, thus demonstrating a growth of style.[3] Smith's 1957 exhibition, sponsored by Ritchie and organized by Sam Hunter, then associate curator of the Department of Painting and Sculpture, included thirty-four sculptures made from 1936 through 1957.

Herman Cherry spent the day of the opening with a very nervous Smith, who was concerned with the way other artists would react to his work. To calm him, Cherry reminded Smith of what he really thought of the Museum of Modern Art.[4] An altercation with a fellow sculptor left Smith even further shaken. When he discovered that Jean's baggage had been stolen, his anxiety burst forth in rage.[5] Jean's parents had given her a new dress to wear at the opening and now it was gone, along with all the other clothes she had brought to New York. She attended the opening in a dress several inches too long, borrowed from the painter Helen Frankenthaler. The long day ended at the Five Spot, a jazz place then favored by many New York artists, on Manhattan's Bowery.[6]

Technically it was not a one-man show, since Echaurren Matta was also being exhibited, but it finally brought Smith both the esteem and the "cashine" he had so long awaited. By the close of the exhibition, Smith had managed to triple his prices over those of the preceding year, and he had sold so many major works that he asked several institutions to stretch their payments over several years because of taxes. By the time the exhibition ended, Yale University, the Brooklyn Museum, Nelson Rockefeller, and the Museum of Modern Art itself had purchased works. The prices brought by those sculptures alone amounted to four times Smith's total income for the year before. Following the Modern's exhibition, no important show of contemporary sculpture anywhere in the world could be considered complete unless Smith were represented.

The exhibition strongly accented Smith's preoccupation during the mid-1950s with vertical forms, which sharply contrasted the earlier emphasis on the horizontal, represented in the show by *Royal Bird* (1948; Fig. 31), *The Fish* (1950), *Australia* (1951; Fig. 32), *The Banquet* (1951; Fig. 34), and *Agricola IX* (1952). The huge, solemn forms of the mid-1950s must have overshadowed his earlier works and almost surely led to a reappraisal of the artist. Some of those pieces, eight feet tall, have the menace of ritualistic monsters and suggest that Smith's interest in symbolism had not disappeared. The totemic forms of the mid-1950s, composed of objects used in daily life, demonstrate the remarkable consistency of Smith's goals. Much earlier, about 1941, he had written, "I am interested in what part of aesthetics represented by the artist's product is controlled by totem recurrencies."[7] One work in the exhibition, *Sitting Printer* of 1954 (Fig. 43), used the back of an oak chair, a stool broken into parts, and a typesetter's box, all of which had been cast in bronze. The result was a strange form that continues to evoke feelings associated with the components in their earlier uses. The typesetter's box is a particularly apt choice both because of its compartmentalized configuration and because of its past use as a container of letter forms. *Sitting Printer's* affinity to *The Letter* (Fig. 27) and *Australian Letter* (Fig. 47) is clear, as is Smith's fascination with the prehistoric origins of language. "Before letters consequently words existed—the artist sculptor made symbols of objects. Pragmatists later made words from the artist symbols and turned them against him."[8]

After leaving the Willard Gallery, Smith decided he should no longer permit any single gallery to represent him. This decision complicated his relations with galleries and museums and worsened his reputation as a difficult man to deal with. In May 1957 Otto Gerson's Fine Arts Associates (FAA) purchased five sculptures, including *Sentinel I*, for a substantial sum and planned a fall exhibition to open the week after the opening of the "Mid-career" show at the Modern. In agreeing to the sale, however, Smith failed to recognize the sense of proprietorship that came with such an acquisition. When Smith shipped *Sentinel I* to the Whitney for its 1958 Annual, Gerson's FAA called the museum several times to make sure it was listed as Smith's dealer. When the Whitney discovered that the selling price had inadvertently been omitted from the catalogue, it called FAA. Smith became so angry at the museum for assuming that FAA was his dealer that he sent a telegram withdrawing the sculpture from exhibition. He apologized later, however, and *Sentinel I* was shown.

Smith and Gerson maintained a stormy relationship over the next several years. Several times they concluded verbal agreements, but each time Smith rejected the written confirmation. He repurchased one sculpture from Gerson, as he did also from the Widdifield Gallery when he got into disagreements with them.

Further complications arose in 1959, when French and Company decided to enter the contemporary field and chose Clement Greenberg as their adviser. French agreed to purchase a major work from Smith and hold two one-man exhibitions for him in successive years, one of paintings and drawings, the other of sculptures. Smith agreed not to raise his prices unless French concurred. Smith stipulated that French was not to act as his general agent. The exhibitions led to a cooling of relations between Greenberg and Smith, which came about when Smith threatened to remove all his sculptures from French after they had been shown because Greenberg had objected to the prices Smith had placed on his paintings at French.[9]

In 1960, in response to French's competition, Gerson offered to purchase between twenty and forty thousand dollars' worth of sculptures each year, thereby relieving Smith of financial worries. Smith refused to commit himself. When Smith then complained about low sales, Gerson, confused, wrote Smith that one day Smith was not interested in selling and the next he was anxious for sales. Gerson offered to ship a group of sculptures to Europe, where FAA had a warehouse and exhibition space.[10] Still Smith refused. In 1961, when FAA purchased seven of his works, Smith wrote, "I hope the purchases you made were on my basis. If they were made with other expectations, I am willing to make amends."[11] He was determined to remain free of any commitments.

Now that Smith had mended his relations with the Museum of Modern Art, he had disagreements with the Whitney. The 1956 damage to *Iron Woman* and Smith's fixing blame on the Whitney's packing has already been cited. A year or two later Lloyd Goodrich, acting in behalf of the Sara Roby Foundation, of which he was a director, decided to purchase Smith's *Cello Player* at the $4,000 price Smith had asked for it when it was shown at the Museum of Modern Art. Smith had already placed it on consignment with a collector, but he wrote that if the collector returned it, the Whitney would get "consideration first."[12] The collector did return it, but now Smith claimed he had asked $5,500 for it. The Whitney declined to raise its offer, and Smith finally agreed to accept the original $4,000 price[13] and deliver the sculpture by Labor Day.[14] Several months after the piece was delivered, Smith complained to Goodrich that he was dissatisfied with the price. He was so dissatisfied, in fact, that he no longer wished to be represented in the Whitney:[15] he wanted to buy back the pieces it had, and he threatened legal action if *Cello Player* were not returned. He also dipped into the past and reminded Goodrich that the Whitney had paid $500 less than the asking price for both *Cockfight* and *Hudson River Landscape*.

Smith's perpetual bickering over prices does not seem to have been prompted by avarice. His letter to Goodrich contains this revealing passage: "The Cello Player is my work. I refuse to accept your offer or any part of its payment. It would not be happy in your care after the rude manner in which you addressed me."[16]

At times, Smith projected his feelings onto his sculptures, and could not bear to think of them in what he considered unfriendly surroundings. This idiosyncrasy may well account for his constant readiness to buy back works from people he suspected of being dissatisfied with them or with him. Constantly rising prices were an indication to him that his own worth was rising, but this feeling was countered by a reluctance to sell the works that were so much a part of him. It was this ambivalence that had confused Otto Gerson and caused him to wonder whether Smith was really interested in selling or not.

If collectors, museums, and galleries learned to be cautious in their dealings with Smith, he had first learned to be wary of them. Though Marian Willard had shielded him from some of the abuses other artists had suffered at their hands, Smith had experienced enough to learn how to defend himself: he became adept at using unfavorable publicity—the same method used by the New York Group to bring pressure on the Metropolitan in 1950.

Smith probably came to recognize the importance of publicity during his advertising experiences at A. G. Spalding and *Tennis* magazine in the late 1920s and early 1930s. Shortly after the "Irascible Eighteen" sent their "open letter" to the *Herald Tribune,* as previously mentioned, Smith planned to have Elaine de Kooning write an article on his work, to coincide with the time when Smith came up for renewal of his Guggenheim fellowship.[17] Smith found another use for the press in 1960, as a way to deal with galleries. A collector purchased *17 h's* from the Castelli Gallery, which had bought the sculpture when it had been shown at the Modern in 1957. The new owner disliked the work's pink paint and ordered it stripped before it was placed in the collection of the University of Arizona at Tucson.[18] Smith then persuaded Thomas Hess, at that time managing editor of *Art News,* to include as part of his monthly editorial a statement about artist's rights.[19] The statement appeared in the May issue, and referred to the incident of Smith's *17 h's.* It pointed out that Smith's only recourse was to repudiate the work. Smith followed the statement with his well-known letter to the editor disavowing *17 h's,* which appeared in the summer issue of *Art News* (Fig. 51) as well as in *Arts* magazine. On August 1, after publication of his letter, Smith wrote to Leo Castelli, asking the work's price should Smith decide to repurchase it.[20] Though Castelli had paid Smith $1,400, he hinted that the collector's purchase price of $3,500 was still well below the market price.[21] On August 7 Smith told Castelli that he would only pay the $1,400 plus 5 percent interest, reminding Castelli that the work had been vandalized and had no market value.[22] In the end, Castelli accepted Smith's $1,400 plus an additional $200.[23]

Smith used the press again in 1961 to register his displeasure with the third prize he was awarded at the Pittsburgh International Exhibition of Contemporary Painting and Sculpture. The incident began with an invitation in October 1960 from Gordon Washburn, then director of the Carnegie Institute's Department of Fine Arts, to participate in the 1961 Pittsburgh exhibition.[24] Smith declined, citing among his reasons the time required to prepare for such competitions and his failure to win previous ones.[25] By March 1961, however, Smith had been persuaded to accept. He set certain conditions: his entry was to be in two parts, one consisting of the sculpture to be judged in the competition and the other a separate exhibition of his works in a room free of paintings that could distract attention from his sculptures. Leon A. Arkus, then assistant director, planned to drive to Bolton Landing to help select the works.[26] Everett Ellin, Smith's West Coast representative, privately, investigated at Smith's request Carnegie's policy on sales commissions.[27]

In August 1961, after a dispute with Gerson over FAA's right to commissions on all

DAVID SMITH

Sir:

Since my sculpture, *17 h's* (44¾ inches high)., 1950, painted Cadmium Aluminum Red, during the process of sale and resale, has suffered a willful act of vandalism [see Editorial, May], I renounce it as my

original work and brand it a ruin.

My name cannot be attributed to it, and I shall exercise my legal rights against anyone making this misrepresentation.

All persons involved in this act of vandalism will be, to the best of my ability, prohibited from acquiring any more of my work.

I declare its value to be only its weight of 60 lbs. of scrap steel.

David Smith
Bolton Landing, N. Y.

Fig. 51. David Smith letter to the editor, *Art News,* Summer 1960. © ARTnews, 1960

sales made on the East Coast, including those at the Pittsburgh International,[28] Smith evidently decided that the only way to thwart Gerson was to sell nothing. Following his usual strategy, he set his prices high enough to discourage the most enthusiastic collector.[29] Unaware of the dispute, Arkus pointed out that Smith's prices were the highest in the show, considerably higher even than Picasso's and would make selling almost impossible. He asked Smith to reconsider,[30] but Smith would not. The museum, Smith decided, was interested in pushing sales in order to offset the cost of shipping with the sales commissions it hoped to collect. So he offered to pay the shipping charges so the museum would not be

134

"stuck" with them.[31] Arkus, no doubt somewhat shocked, managed to mollify Smith enough to elicit an apology from him.

As usual, Smith wanted to display all of his works together in one group. He wrote Arkus, "Do not take favorably to separation, having some in hall, would rather be crowded and all together in one room."[32] Accordingly, all of the sculptures that could be fitted were, in Arkus's words, "jam-packed" into the room. *Two Box Structure*, was, however, too tall and had to be put in the hallway; *Dida's Circle on a Fungus* fitted nowhere and had to be returned to Bolton Landing.[33]

On October 24, 1961, a letter from Gordon Washburn informed Smith that his *Zig IV* had won him the $1,000 third prize for sculpture.[34] Smith promptly proclaimed that the award system was archaic and rejected his prize. A few days later his letter of rejection was published in the *New York Times* and was referred to in an article critical of the award system by John Canaday, then the *Times* art critic (Fig. 52). Smith's rejection came a little late. As Leon Arkus has pointed out,[35] Smith could have entered his works *hors de concours*, an option he failed to exercise. Apparently Smith's feelings were bruised by the awarding of second prize to George Sugarman, at that time a relatively unknown artist.[36] In a letter to James Truitt, a newsman and friend, Smith summarized the situation succinctly: "Was Pittsburg & back—got 3d prize refused it at once. 3d class virtue I don't want—rather be old whore. Will stay out of competitions now."[37] In the end Smith took the money and managed to save face at the same time, thanks to a stratagem devised by Arkus. To settle the problem of what to do with the money after Smith had returned it, Arkus

SCULPTOR REJECTS AWARD OF $1,000

David Smith Won 3d Prize at Carnegie International

PITTSBURGH, Oct. 31 (UPI)—An official of the Carnegie Institute declined comment today on the refusal of a sculptor to accept a $1,000 prize for his entry in the institute's international Exhibition of Contemporary Painting an Sculpture.

The sculptor, David Smith of Bolton Landing, N. Y., wrote a letter to the institute rejecting the third prize awarded his work, "Zig IV," a three-dimensional non-objective work done in iron.

Gordon Washburn, director of the institute's Department of Fine Arts, who made the selections in the show, had little to say about Mr. Smith's action.

"We'd just as soon not have it publicized," he said. "Smith's letter has not yet been referred to the attention of the institute's trustees, who meet in about a month."

The exhibition also is displaying Mr. Smith's one-man show of his welded sculptures, including "Zigs I, II, III and V." His "Zig IV" is priced at $45,000. According to the show's price list, the other "Zigs" range in price from $32,000 to $45,000, which makes Mr. Smith the highest price artist in the show.

Since the International opened last Friday, 104 pieces of sculpture and paintings have been sold for $179,470.

Calls System 'Archaic'

Reached last night at his home, Mr. Smith said he had rejected the Pittsburgh prize because he believed that the system of awarding honors in 1-2-3-4-5 fashion was "archaic" and "undemocratic."

The sculptor emphasized that his act of rejection was done with a feeling of complete friendliness between himself and the jury and Mr. Washburn. He said that he did not feel that a jury was in a position to say that one man was better than another, within certain limits, and he suggested that instead of prizes being awarded to individuals, the money should be used to purchase the works of art for museum display.

The selection of honor works of art in the show was criticized last Friday by John Canaday, the art critic of The New York Times. Mr. Canaday said that "the ways of juries are always a puzzle, but this one seems to have gone out of its way to confuse."

Mr. Canaday observed that Mr. Smith, "a top man, came out at the bottom" with his "Zig IV."

Fig. 52. "Sculptor Rejects Award of $1,000," *New York Times*, November 1, 1961. © 1961 by The New York Times Company. Reprinted by permission

offered to buy a Smith drawing that he had seen during his stay at Bolton Landing for $1,000, the amount of the award. Smith replied that it was too much; he would give two. When Arkus received the package, it contained four Smith drawings: two from Smith and one each in the names of his daughters as gifts to the museum.[38]

Although in this instance his generosity won him a small personal coup over a museum, it was not always a means to a personal end. Smith could be remarkably helpful to other artists. He had introduced James Rosati to Otto Gerson and later persuaded Gerson to represent Rosati. When Smith learned that neither Kenneth Noland nor Morris Louis had been invited to exhibit works in the Pittsburgh International, he wrote a strong letter recommending that they be considered. When they still failed to receive invitations, he wrote again. As a consequence of Smith's recommendation, Gordan Washburn planned to review Louis's work for possible acceptance, and although neither artist was represented in the exhibition, Arkus took note of them as artists.[39]

When Herman Cherry needed a serious back operation and lacked the money to pay for it, Smith was again successful in his generous efforts to help. He went to Philip Guston and Willem de Kooning, explained the situation, and asked each of them to contribute two drawings. He then took their four drawings and two of his own to Cherry's gallery and sold them. A considerable sum was left over after the hospital bill was paid, but none of the three would accept any of it so Cherry used the money to throw a gigantic party. The announcements were sent out under the names of Cherry's three friends, Cherry having refused to let his own name be used. At one time or another over the course of that night more than a thousand people celebrated in a loft under de Kooning's studio at Twelfth Street and Broadway. The last of the throng finally went home at 5 A.M., long after the liquor and food had disappeared.[40]

By the beginning of the 1960s, when Smith was making his mature work, he had less inclination to bristle quickly. Younger artists found him sympathetic and willing to help if he thought them worthy. As his clashes with Otto Gerson and Clement Greenberg indicated, he could still be unreasonable and quick to anger over what he felt were insults, though the explosions were less violent and less frequent than they had been. In part the hunger for success that had driven him during the 1940s and 1950s had slackened. But also the museum and gallery directors who had either experienced his anger or been forewarned by the experiences of others had learned to approach him with caution.

In 1959 Emily Genauer attended the exhibition of Smith paintings at French and Company. Seeing the luminous pinks and grays, she wondered whether after all the years of "bristling rusty iron arrangements," he was going soft. Dorothy Miller also noticed the mellowing attitude. As Alfred Barr's representative she had been on the receiving end of Smith's anger toward the museum and Alfred Barr in the forties and fifties. When she saw Smith in 1964, shortly before he was to present a large number of his "Cubi" sculptures at the Marlborough-Gerson Gallery, he generously offered to lend the museum three "Cubis" for its newly reopened sculpture garden which the museum gladly accepted. She thought at that time that he looked sad and lonely.[41]

Unfortunately, Smith had mellowed too late to save his marriage. Jean had endured almost daily bouts of violence before she finally left Smith in 1958.[42] Herman Cherry had tried to warn him that Jean needed greater consideration and a change from Bolton Landing, but he apparently did not heed the warning. He still attempted to control Jean even after their divorce. One way was through money. In a letter to Jean in early February 1965 Smith complained that he was so short of money that he could not even meet the week's payroll, yet records show that he was holding a check in the amount of $28,000, which he did not deposit until several weeks after he had received it.[43] Jean had to go to court in order to collect child support. Once when he was threatened with jail for nonsupport, Smith tried to find out how long the sentence was likely to be.

Yet he loved his children deeply. When they were with him, he was almost prudish in his protectiveness. He bored his friends with his endless talk about them. Many sculptures were dedicated to Rebecca and Candida. His daughters were also a factor in Smith's reluctance to sell his sculptures. He correctly sensed that his work would continue to increase in value, and at times preferred to pass up opportunities for sales, confident that his daughters would eventually benefit. Despite the urgings of friends, however, Smith refused to give sculptures to the children during his lifetime. In a sense, the sculptures were Smith's real offspring, the only ones he could really control.

In November 1960 Smith attended the opening of his first West Coast one-man exhibition, at the Everett Ellin Gallery in Los Angeles. His work was well received and over $17,000 worth of sculpture was sold by January 1961. Encouraged, Ellin went to Dallas in June, where he contacted more than forty collectors, some of them clients of Otto Gerson. In Fort Worth and Saint Louis, he showed Gerson clients photographs of new works that Gerson himself had not yet seen. Gerson was angered, but he could do nothing to stop Ellin's activity, for his relationship with Smith was ambiguous. He had never succeeded in obtaining exclusive representation, and Smith resented Gerson's efforts to pin him down.

West Coast sales were excellent in 1962 and the Smith-Ellin relationship blossomed. It enabled Smith to adopt a more independent attitude toward Gerson and continue to raise his prices. In May 1962 Ellin expanded into larger new quarters. Unfortunately, the West Coast market was limited for works in Smith's price bracket, and by mid-1963 sales had decreased so much that Ellin had to close his gallery and return east. Smith, now without a West Coast representative, had his works shipped back to Bolton Landing.[44]

In spring 1962 the composer Gian-Carlo Menotti invited Smith to take part in the Festival of Two Worlds at Spoleto, Italy, during that June. Reluctant to leave Bolton Landing for an entire month, Smith declined, even though Menotti offered him the use of a factory and all the supplies he might need. Menotti persisted: what could he offer Smith that would change his mind? Smith's answer: the dedication of an opera to Rebecca and Candida. Menotti agreed.

On his arrival in Italy, carrying drawings of sculptures he planned to make, Smith was offered the use of an abandoned factory in Voltri and six workers. With so many helpers, Smith had an opportunity to work on a scale of which he had earlier only dreamed. During the thirty days of the festival, Smith and his crew (none of whom spoke English) produced twenty-six major works that astounded and delighted the director of the exhibition, Giovanni Carandente. Because of their size and number, Carandente had the sculptures placed in the ancient coliseum at Spoleto, a decision that greatly pleased Smith.

The Voltri environment was congenial to Smith, thanks to the generosity of the Italian government and the warmth of Carandente. The factory recalled childhood incidents as well as the Terminal Iron Works on the Brooklyn waterfront. Its forges and hand tongs reminded him of the distant past in Decatur, Indiana, and the not-so-distant past at the blacksmith shop in Bloomington. He covered a steel layout table with lime so that the dark components of his sculptures stood out as strongly against the white surface as they did on the white-painted garage floor at Bolton Landing.

Despite his pleasure with the working conditions at Voltri, however, Smith was troubled by a lack of the proper supplies. The factory that was to produce the stainless steel he had planned to use had not yet begun production and no supply was available. His recent Bolton Landing work had made heavy use of modular forms of stainless steel, and it is reasonable to assume that the drawings he brought with him were based on similar ideas. The first work, *Voltri I* (Fig. 53), in Smith's words "came desperately." It reflected Smith's intention to continue in the direction begun with his modular constructions, even without stainless steel. Its tentativeness contrasts with the boldness of sculptures made at Bolton Landing and manifests the concern Smith admitted feeling. Evidently dissatisfied with the result, he abandoned the modular format and turned his attention to the tools left about in the old factory. He could make nothing with them, but perhaps he could make something of them.

He spent several anxious days shuffling the old tools around. Their forms, with their eccentric appearances and scuffed, uneven surfaces, were quite different from the relatively cold perfection of the stainless-steel modules he worked with at Bolton Landing. They were much closer in feeling to the idiosyncratic shapes that had formed part of Smith's early oeuvre at the Terminal Iron Works. Thus it was logical for him to turn back as he did to sources earlier than the "Cubi" series for his images. The "Tanktotems," whose scuffed, eccentric forms resembled those of the old tools at Voltri, represented a continuity of thinking from the Brooklyn days and were the most recent source on which Smith drew for his images. For the "Tanktotems," however, Smith had had to cut and weld in order to develop the eccentricity that already existed in the Voltri factory tools.

Several old impulses are renewed in the works Smith produced at Voltri. The dominant theme, as it had been since *The Letter* of 1950, was the combining of male and female symbols in a violent relationship that was characterized by repeated violations of circular forms by steel bars of various shapes. Smith's second Voltri work, *Voltri II* (Fig. 54), set the precedent for the development of that theme in many of the subsequent "Voltri" and "Voltri-Bolton" sculptures and foreshadowed *Circle I, II,* and *III* (Fig. 55) made in fall 1962. In other works, such as *Voltri XV* (Fig. 56) and *Voltri XII* (Fig. 57), Smith brought back his familiar image of the female as predator, piercing the rings with clawlike forms. He also returned to the stage settings he had used so often during the 1940s as a means of organizing forms, but with an important difference. The earlier platforms had served only the utilitarian purpose of supporting the forms; in the Voltri sculptures the platforms

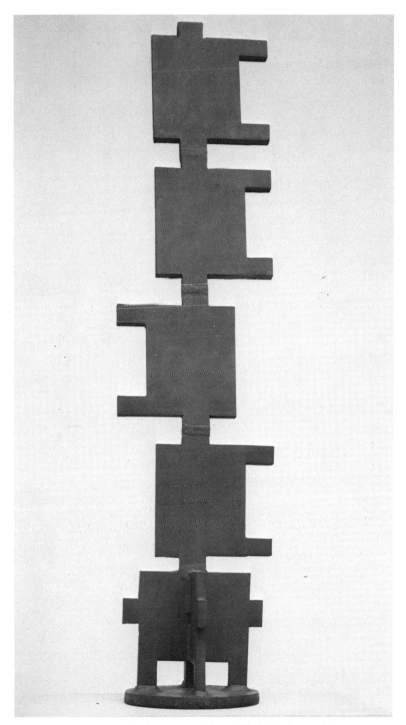

Fig. 53. *Voltri I,* 1962. Steel. 92⅞ × 22⅛ × 19″. Collection and photo courtesy Hirshhorn Museum and Sculpture Garden, Smithsonian Institution, Washington, D.C.

Fig. 54. *Voltri I* and *II*, 1962. Steel. *II*, 70 × 40½ × 15″. Collection Giovanni Carandente, Spoleto, Italy. Photo by Publifoto, Genoa, courtesy Candida and Rebecca Smith

140

Fig. 55. *Circle I, II, III,* 1962. Painted steel. 74 × 105 × 16″, 101½ × 112 × 15⅞″, 95½ × 72 × 18″. Collection and photo courtesy National Gallery of Art, Washington, D.C.

Fig. 56. *Voltri XV,* 1962. Steel. 89⅜ × 77½ × 23″. Collection Hirshhorn Museum and Sculpture Garden, Smithsonian Institution, Washington, D.C. Photo by David Smith

Fig. 57. *Voltri XII,* 1962. Steel. 87 × 47¾ × 13½″. Collection and photo courtesy Mr. and Mrs. Gilbert H. Kinney, Washington, D.C.

Fig. 58. *Voltri VII,* 1962. Steel. 83¾ × 122½ × 44½″. Collection National Gallery of Art, Washington, D.C. Ailsa Mellon Bruce Fund. Photo by David Smith

144

became part of the imagery. Spectators no longer had mentally to block out the lower section of a sculpture; now the entire work was a single integrated image. The base of *Voltri VII* (Fig. 58) was an old foundry cart that still functioned, so Smith dubbed the piece his "chariot." Every object in the Voltri factory had the potential of being transformed through Smith's ingenuity. When a variety of old implements were left over after he had completed the twenty-six festival works and another called *Voltri Doll,* he crated them and shipped them to Bolton Landing. There he made twenty-five additional sculptures, the "Voltri-Bolton" series.

During the fall of 1962 Smith's relations with Gerson continued to deteriorate. Smith found fault with the way several drawings had been packed and demanded that all of them be returned from the gallery. He refused Gerson's request for photographs; because of lack of time and proper help he could not be bothered[45]—this he said to the dealer who the previous year had sold over $44,000 worth of his sculpture, $16,000 of which Gerson purchased for his own account.

In December 1962 Otto Gerson died without having negotiated a written contract with Smith. His efforts to follow up verbal agreements with written ones had failed repeatedly. Gerson knew that Smith often disregarded verbal agreements. Yet a part of the problem lay in Gerson's failure to understand Smith. Smith's apparent weakness in face-to-face confrontations would tend to make him fearful of letting any dealer achieve a dominant position. Gerson's aggressive business techniques made Smith wary. Yet Smith needed Gerson: he was working at an unprecedented pace. With Gerson gone, who could be found with the scope of operations and the financial strength to cope with the prodigious amount of work coming from Bolton Landing?

Smith found his answer in 1963, when the Marlborough Galleries took over FAA and created Marlborough-Gerson. In April, Frank Lloyd, the owner of the combined galleries, began efforts to obtain a written agreement with Smith. At last Smith had no real alternative, and an exclusive agreement was signed in fall 1963. One consequence of that agreement was the mammoth exhibition of Smith sculptures which took place at Marlborough-Gerson in October 1964. Scale had always been an obsession of Smith's. This exhibition, the last major one before his death, must have satisfied it. In it were no fewer than eight "Cubi" sculptures and two of the huge "Zig" series. The massive works were hoisted up the outside of the building and through a special folding window that had been provided on the sixth floor. Since it was impossible to move the sculptures down to the fifth-floor storage area, after the exhibition they were removed in the same way. Even the table-sized "Menands" were cut from thick steel plates, their light and graceful curves giving no hint of their tremendous weight. It was an eclectic show, as any representative Smith exhibition had to be. The rusted "Menands" contrasted with the lost-wax bronze planes, and neither bore any obvious relationship to the polished stainless-steel "Cubis" and the painted "Zigs." Smith's work did not readily lend itself to categorizing: he could comfortably work concurrently in several styles, techniques, and materials.

11

THE LATE WORK

After 1957, Smith fully developed his method of working in series. In them we can discern a consistency, a coalescing of direction, that was not apparent in his earlier work. Smith was not particularly concerned with the idea of style, per se. Rather it was the sources and shapes of the materials which became the basis of a series, the link between works. The Y-shaped forms from a hardware store, for example, suggested letters and led to *24 Greek Y's* (Fig. 35), *17 h's* (Fig. 36) and, of course, *The Letter* (Fig. 27). The dish-shaped ends of tanks led to the "Tanktotem" series, farm implements to "Agricola," and the heavy metal plates from Albany Steel and Iron Supply to the "Albany" series.

There were two chief sources of the cohesiveness. The use of welded modular forms after 1950 was the first. Despite his inventiveness in using and creating irregular forms, the result, as we have seen, was a substantially more geometrical art than the idiosyncratic one of the 1940s, which was a product of combining a variety of techniques and materials. The second and later source of consistency lay in Smith's eventual grasp of the possibilities inherent in the reworking and refining of basic images. *Circle I, II,* and *III,* made in fall 1962, picked up the theme of the "Voltri" works, which in turn had adapted previously used sexual symbols. In each instance the image became further distilled without being vitiated. I believe that by distilling a limited number of repeatable images, Smith was able to develop in his work a consistency and maturity that contrasted markedly with the conglomeration of unrelated ideas and forms which characterized his earlier sculpture, such as the "table-top tableaux." It is worth pausing here to see how one format, wheeled constructions, was refined until it became part of the imagery.

The first of the wheeled constructions, *Sentinel III* (1957; Fig. 59), is a configuration that mixes the image of the totem with those of conveyence (the tricycle) and voyage (the sail). The base's three-wheeled structure is inventive but contextually unrelated to the upper segment. The construction was better suited to Smith's early eclectic style than to the serial development he was initiating at that time. The tripod arrangement is a variation of a device that Smith had been using for several years (see *Portrait of a Painter,* Fig. 44, and *Portrait of a Lady Painter,* Fig. 45) to circumvent the need to stabilize a tall form with a heavy base, the mass of which would tend to separate it visually from the upper section (see *The Hero,* Fig. 40). Affixed to *Sentinel III's* topmost part is the saillike form that reinforces the idea of

Fig. 59. *Sentinel III,* 1957. Painted steel. 83¾ × 27 × 16¼". Collection Stephen D. Paine, Boston. Photo by David Smith

motion we get from the wheels, but its success in integrating top and bottom is limited. The sliced I-beams represent Smith's most innovative use of modules up to that time. Still hesitant to stretch his forms sideways, to orient his work horizontally, Smith clung to the totem idea, piling his forms one on top of another as he retreated to the central axis of his earlier work.

Zig IV (Fig. 60), the only wheeled "Zig" of the five made in 1961, is powerful in its use of modules but still fails to integrate base and superstructure. The utilitarian advantage of making a massive form mobile is clear—so clear, in fact, that it almost seems as though Smith had no other wish than to avoid having to slip a trucker's dolly under the sculpture when he wanted to move it and so permanently attached one to it. Once again Smith made only a limited effort to integrate top and bottom, this time by covering *Zig IV* with a unifying coat of paint.

The power of *Zig IV* becomes clear only at that point above the base where the viewer's eye is arrested by the inclined steel plane. The sheer breadth of the platform overwhelms the structure beneath,[1] relegating the horizontal plane of the "dolly" to the status of a support member; this feeling is reinforced by the small wheels. The platform recalls the "table-top tableaux" of the 1940s. In the earlier works, however, the platforms were horizontal planes, stages for figurative dramas. By inclining the massive surface, Smith succeeded in making it an active part of the sculpture. Unfortunately, the tilting that strengthened the platform as a sculptural element also exposed the weak underside (Fig. 61). The several meaningless components attached to the underside are obvious efforts to compensate for that weakness. Since Smith did not again use the tilted plane, we may assume that he considered the problem essentially unsolvable.

Zig IV's platform illustrates clearly Smith's growing sensitivity to parts of his sculptures which he had previously considered merely functional. Not until the month in Voltri did he turn that sensitivity toward the wheels. It was there that the platform and wheels became integrated with the body of the sculpture. At Voltri one of his early plans was to mount a sculpture on an old railroad flatcar in such a way that they would combine as a single work. (One can imagine Smith's pleasure at the thought of his railroad sculpture being drawn grandly into the piazza at Spoleto, while the other artists gasped.) Though the flatcar idea proved impractical, it awakened Smith to the image-making possibilities of wheeled sculptures, and his attention was drawn to the carts that had been used to transport forgings from the oven to the drop hammer. Of those "chariots" Smith wrote:

> Circles have long been a preoccupation, more primary than squares. Wheels are circles with mobility, from the first wheel of man, to wheels on Indian stone temples, . . . to all the suns and poetic imagery of movement to the practical fact that my sculpture is getting too big to move without built in rolling: Voltri VI is a tong with wheels and two end clouds one cloud rests in the spoon—each cloud end goes up from the tongue unsupported. Voltri VII is a chariot ram with 5 bar forgings—they are not personages—they are forgings. Voltri XIII is a circus wheel chariot with the spoon turned over, a solid guitar forging with a punched hole— with cloud parts below and above its tongue.[2]

Fig. 60. *Zig IV,* 1961. Painted steel. 94⅞ × 84¼ × 76½″. Collection and photo courtesy Vivian Beaumont Theater, Lincoln Center for the Performing Arts, New York. Photo by David Smith

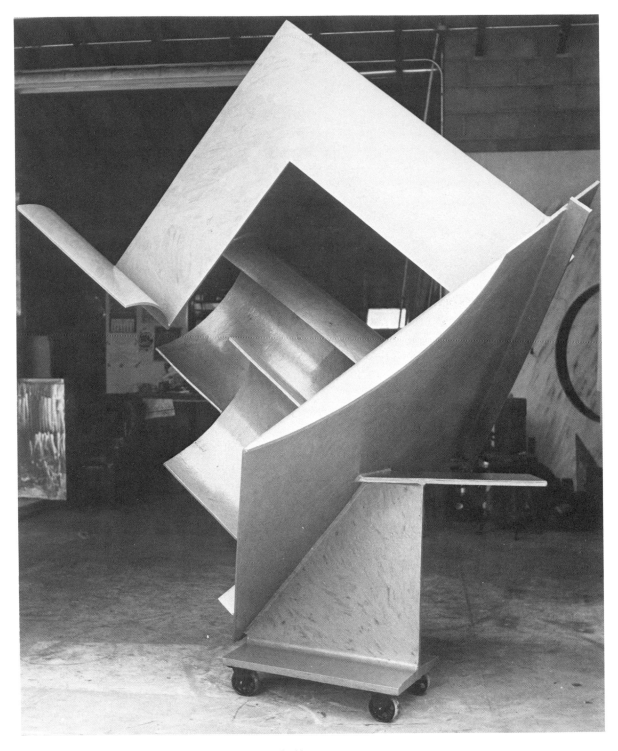

Fig. 61. Underside of *Zig IV.* Photo by David Smith

150

Of the four "Voltri" vehicles, three—*Voltri VI* (1962; Fig. 62), *Voltri VII* (1962; Fig. 58), and *Voltri XIII* (1962; Fig. 63)—were of narrow-gauge construction and significantly linked to the three "Wagons" of 1964. The fourth, *Voltri XVIII*, a broad-platformed vehicle, is a direct reworking of *Zig IV*, though its flat bed makes it much less dynamic. In the first three, Smith deliberately strung his forms along the shallow platforms of the carts to create frontal planes. In each, the stationary support below the platform was transformed into an integral part of the sculpture by its placement within the same frontal plane as the upper forms, as was one wheel. The wheels, because of their frontal positions, their size, their complexity, and the scuffed surfaces that relate them to other components are found objects as well as supports. The platforms no longer are bases but act as dividers to separate upper and lower forms. The lower section of *Voltri XIII* is even more complex than the upper, so that the frontality of the entire sculpture is reinforced, not just that of its upper portion.

The Spoleto experience unquestionably influenced Smith to rethink not only the possibilities of wheeled sculptures but also those of scale. With the relatively large number of workers at his disposal in Italy, Smith was able to expand greatly the size and weight of his works, which opened to him the idea of working on a larger scale back home. The three sculptures of the "Wagon" series seem directly catalyzed by his Italian experience.

So massive are the parts of the "Wagons" that they had to be cast at a commercial foundry, American Forge in McKees Rock, Pennsylvania. Of the three works, *Wagon II* (1964, Fig. 64)[3] is the heaviest and, in fact, the heaviest sculpture he ever made. Its total weight is so great that the lift on Smith's pickup truck, which supposedly had a capacity of eight tons, could not lift it.[4] Smith obtained its wheels (and those of *Wagon I*) from Bethlehem Steel shortly after his return from Spoleto, asking for wheels of unusual size and weight. Three of *Wagon II*'s wheels, each weighing 275 pounds, had been originally intended to bear the weight of a hundred-ton trolley car. It is the gigantic fourth wheel, however, that draws the viewer's attention: it was made from five separate steel plates welded together and bored at the axle. Sketches for the tongues and yokes of the wagons were sent to American Forge. By April 1964 some 3,800 pounds of forged mild steel had been shipped to Bolton Landing at a cost of $1,290.

Wagon II's spine (Fig. 65) was to be roughly fashioned. (Smith had instructed American Forge to give all the forgings a "rough and raw" finish; deviations and forge marks would be acceptable with a tolerance of plus or minus 30 percent. He wanted the tongue assembly of *Wagon II* to have an "old-style blacksmith look.") The spine arrived at Bolton Landing with a straight yoke end, which Leon Pratt heated with a torch until it could be bent over the yoke. The massive hook that was thus formed was then filled with weld metal. The vertical form in the center of the spine was a rejected railroad coupling from Bethlehem Steel and created a feeling similar to that of the vertical elements of *Voltri III*. The rear axle of *Wagon II* (upper section, Fig. 66) was unbalanced to accommodate the massive back wheel. Another sketch (lower section, Fig. 66) for a similar but square axle was evidently either never built or else not used.

It is likely that Figure 67 was intended as a blueprint for *Wagon I* although it calls for a

Fig. 62. *Voltri VI,* 1962. Steel. 98 × 103¼ × 25½". Collection Mr. and Mrs. Raymond D. Nasher. Photo by David Smith

152

Fig. 63. *Voltri XIII,* 1962. Steel. 64⅛ × 103¾ × 26″. Collection University Art Museum, University of California at Berkeley. Gift of Mr. and Mrs. Eugene E. Trefethen, Jr., Piedmont, California. Photo by David Smith

Fig. 64. *Wagon II,* 1964. Steel. 107½ × 111¼ × 44″. Collection Candida and Rebecca Smith. Photo by Ugo Mulas

154

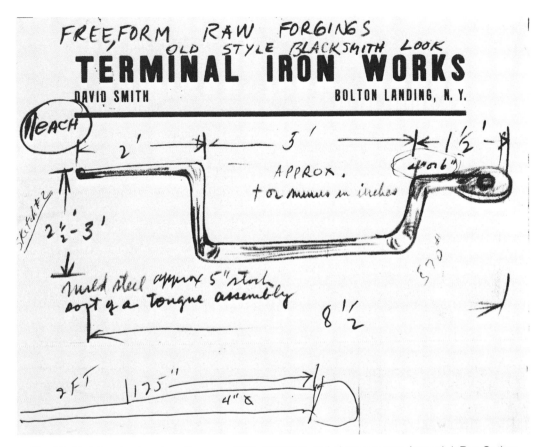

Fig. 65. Sketches for American Forge, c. 1964. Collection and photo courtesy Aaronel deRoy Gruber

shallower curve, tapered at both ends, than what finally emerged. The sketches for the axles appear in Figure 68 and the upper section of Figure 69. *Wagon I*'s wheels were also intended originally for use on a trolley. At the bottom of Figure 69 appears the sketch for the twisted spine that eventually became part of *Wagon III*. Smith evidently decided to have wheels for *Wagon III* cast to his own specifications. Figure 70 shows that they were to be heavily tapered; they were either never made or never put to use.

From the sketches we can see that Smith made continual reference to a raw, unfinished look in the pieces. The evidence of manufacture remains on the coarse, hammered surfaces. The crude forms seem to have been hand-crafted for some elusive purpose. *Wagon II* evokes fanciful images (perhaps a rider in a carriage) but also still retains the spirit of forms that were once purely functional.

The use of wheels in *Zig VIII* (1965; Fig. 71) results in a sculpture that is very different from *Zig IV* and *Wagon II*. The wheels are small, like those of *Zig IV*, but by continuing to tilt the platform until it becomes the frontal plane, Smith has completely exposed them. The power thus added to the support section has turned this work into a vehicular sculpture

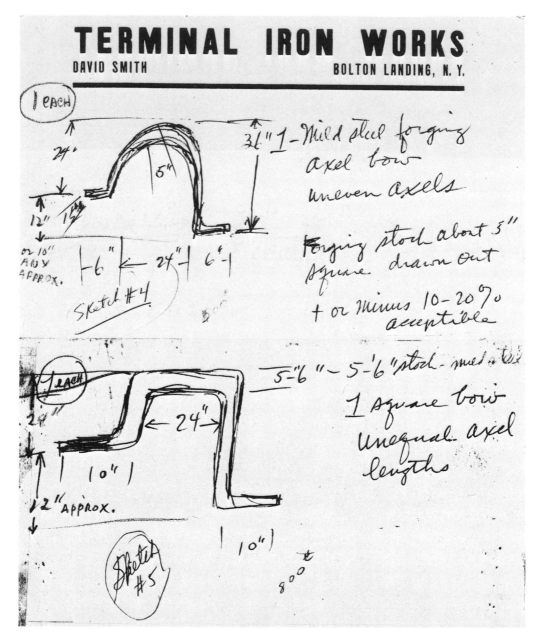

Fig. 66. Sketches for American Forge, c. 1964. Collection and photo courtesy Aaronel deRoy Gruber

rather than a sculpture with built-in dolly. By comparison, *Wagon II*'s massive wheels make it more readily recognizable as a vehicle than as a sculpture.

The development of Smith's wheeled constructions was complex. The step from *Sentinel III*'s wheeled support to that of *Zig VIII* does not seem very great, yet, because of his experiences at Voltri, Smith's attitude toward wheels became nearly reverential. The

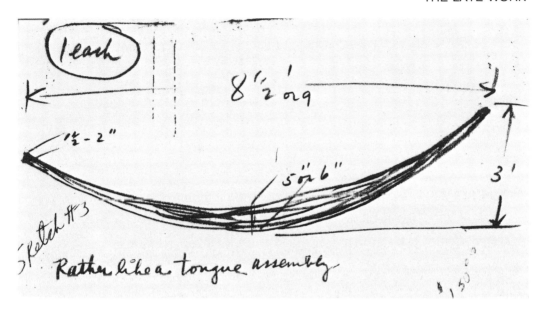

1 each

8½′ org

1½ - 2″

5″ 6″

3′

Sketch #3

Rather like a tongue assembly

Fig. 67. Sketches for American Forge, c. 1964. Collection and photo courtesy Aaronel deRoy Gruber

"Voltri" carts had awakened in Smith a deep feeling of kinship with artisans of the past. Of equal importance was Smith's awareness that he must pay attention to all parts of his sculptures. He resolved to permit no "dead" areas. Forms that previously had only a functional purpose of supporting his images now came to function as images themselves. The consistency among the wheeled constructions derived not from the wheels but from a steadily growing recognition of ways in which they could serve as images. Smith came to use wheels, like musical instruments, to convey a variety of otherwise inexpressible feelings.

Smith had always been concerned about the surface treatment of his sculptures. For many years that concern was a practical one. Despite the tendency of mild steel to rust—particularly in New York City, where acidic vapors speed the process—Smith chose to work in it because it was cheaper than more durable stainless steel. In the late 1930s he began to investigate surface treatments that would provide protective coatings. At the same time he began to experiment with various patinas in search of effective ways to introduce color. As his works grew in number and size, the storage problem forced him to pay still more attention to the protection of surfaces. At first he applied heavy coatings of grease, but this method was time consuming and costly. By the early 1950s he was producing works in such large quantity and scale that he was forced to store them in the fields of Bolton Landing. Smith had to find ways of preserving the sculptures' surfaces from the elements before they were irreparably damaged.

The method he came to use most frequently was to let the sculptures rust for a season, remove the scales with a wire brush, and then coat the surfaces with Masury oil.[5] This method not only preserved the surfaces but gave them a dark reddish color that added

157

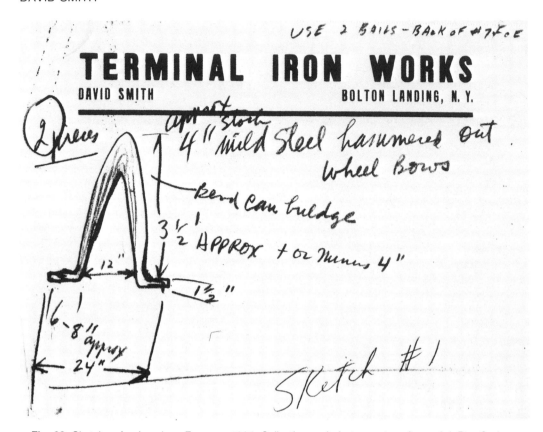

Fig. 68. Sketches for American Forge, c. 1964. Collection and photo courtesy Aaronel deRoy Gruber

another dimension to their imagery. ''The red of rust has a higher value to me than antiquity relationship. . . . It is the red of the easts mythical west—It is the blood of man, it was one culture symbol of life.''[6]

An alternative protective coating, paint, created serious problems of both maintenance and aesthetics. Smith may well have tried every available primer on the market. An airtight bond had to be maintained between steel and paint to prevent deterioration. If moisture seeped in—through a scratch, for example—the paint tended to lift and eventually slough off. It was not unusual for Smith to apply as many as thirty or forty coats of paint in an effort to protect the metal surface from scratches. Some sculptures, such as *Zig IV*, were left in their primer coats. The primer in that instance was P-70 Pri-Met, developed by a Brooklyn firm to protect ships' bottoms from barnacles during World War II. The P-70 was extremely durable; even the heat from a welding torch failed to blister it.[7] Smith sometimes gave a sculpture seven or eight coats of P-70 and one or two of white alkyd flat primer before applying multiple coats of automobile paint. When a slough nevertheless developed, repair proved very difficult. Because the sculptures were in the sun, their colors faded and became impossible to match. The alternative was to apply a completely new coat of paint.

158

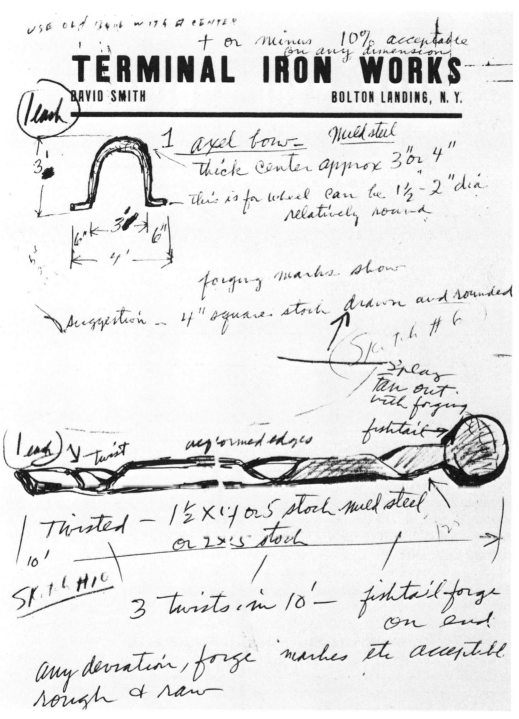

USE OLD BAND WITH A CENTER

+ or minus 10% acceptable on any dimension

TERMINAL IRON WORKS

DAVID SMITH   BOLTON LANDING, N.Y.

(1 each)

1 axel bow — Mild steel
thick center approx 3" or 4"
this is for wheel can be 1½-2" dia
relatively round

forging marks show

suggestion — 4" square stock drawn and rounded

Sketch # 6

spear
fan out
with forging
fishtail

(1 each) Y twist   unformed edges

Twisted — 1½ × 1'4 or .5 stock mild steel
or 2×.5 stock

10'

SKETCH 10

3 twists in 10' — fishtail forge on end

any deviation, forge marks etc acceptable
rough & raw

Fig. 69. Sketches for American Forge, c. 1964. Collection and photo courtesy Aaronel deRoy Gruber

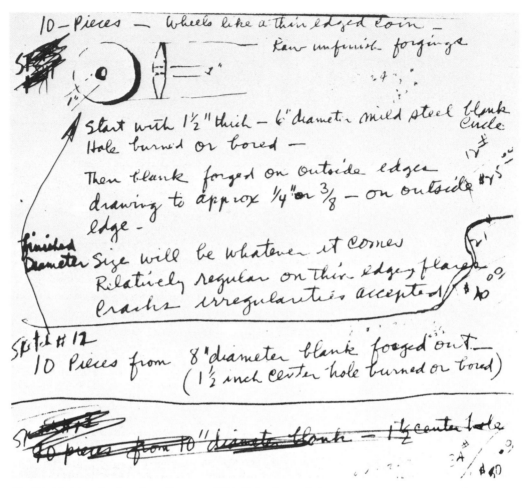

10 – Pieces – Wheels like a thin edged coin –
– Raw unfinish forgings

Start with 1½" thick – 6" diameter mild steel blank Circle.
Hole burned or bored –

Then blank forged on outside edges
drawing to approx ¼" or ⅜ – on outside
edge –

finished
Diameter Size will be whatever it comes
Relatively regular on thin edges flange
cracks irregularities accepted

Sketch #12
10 Pieces from 8" diameter blank forged out.
(1½ inch center hole burned or bored)

10 pieces from 10" diameter blank – 1½ center hole

Fig. 70. Sketches for American Forge, c. 1964. Collection and photo courtesy Aaronel deRoy Gruber

The scaled section, however, always remained depressed even after the edges had been sanded smooth, so that the surface was uneven. These repair problems made exhibitions a trial for Smith. Large sculptures had to be handled gingerly lest the paint be chipped, and workmen were required to wear gloves to prevent leaving finger marks.

There were the aesthetic difficulties also. For example, the color of works painted with P-70 was limited to yellow, the only color the paint came in. The feathering on the ocher surface of *Zig IV* seems to have been at least partly an effort to relieve the severity of the zinc chromate primer. Other than through the imitation of natural color, polychromed surfaces of sculpture have not proved aesthetically successful. We are so accustomed to the simulation of three-dimensional forms on canvas through the use of colors that it is a critical problem to find some other logic for color construction on sculpture. Smith was not the artist to find it. But he would never admit defeat. In 1964 he optimistically wrote to

Fig. 71. *Zig VIII*, 1965. Painted steel. 100¾ × 91½ × 83″. Collection and photo courtesy Museum of Fine Arts, Boston. Centennial Purchase Fund

Clement Greenberg: "Painting on later painted pieces more satisfactory. . . . whichever the case may be solid color is too easy and not my challenge."[8] Here we see the same blend of optimism and stubbornness that he displayed in 1936 when he wrote to Edgar Levy from Europe that his work was improving and his painting was "getting level." He never managed to become a painter, but his polychromed sculptures bear witness to his continued interest in the art of using color.

The problems Smith encountered in his attempts to keep the surfaces of his works from deteriorating made him yearn for the time when he could afford stainless steel: it finally came in 1957. The Museum of Modern Art exhibition provided Smith with enough money to begin full-scale use of stainless steel. As its characteristics are so different from those of mild steel, however, Smith's working methods necessarily changed, and with them the nature of his art.

Smith used T-304, an Austenitic stainless steel, exclusively. It is highly resistant to corrosion and has excellent welding characteristics. Its great advantage to Smith was its 18 to 20 percent chromium content, which creates a chromium oxide skin. The skin forms a protective coating and keeps the appearance lustrous even under urban grime (as long as the atmosphere is oxidizing; in a reducing atmosphere, the skin breaks down). That same chromium content has its drawbacks, however. It is much more refractory than other components of Austenitic stainless, and under high temperatures it migrates to the surface and forms a protective sac around the molten metal, not unlike a plastic bag filled with water. When Leon Pratt tried to cut it with his oxyacetylene torch, designed for use on mild steel, it would only "melt and blow."[9]

Because the shearing resistance of stainless is twice that of mild steel, and plate thicknesses over a quarter-inch frequently tear and break when they are cut cold, Smith could not cut it with either a torch or mechanical methods. Without any way of cutting stainless steel in his shop, he was forced to buy it precut by his fabricator, Ryerson Steel. Unusual shapes could not be ordered since the quantities would have been too small for a production line. So Smith had to limit himself to basic geometric configurations. To work creatively with materials at hand, he needed a large assortment of various shapes and sizes—an assortment that he could not begin to accumulate until his financial situation was better than it ever was before the Modern exhibition established his reputation.

The welding of stainless steel also presented problems. The chromium oxide skin made oxyacetylene welding very difficult. Smith could and did use an arc welder, since its intense heat could break through the skin. The flux that coats the rod is used to dissolve the oxide formed by the heat. The rod, as it welds, is consumed and leaves a deposit of metal that constantly builds up and must be removed. An alternative is a heli-arc welder, and Smith bought one in the early 1960s. With this method a cone of inert gas, usually argon, surrounds the area being welded and prevents oxygen from entering. The chromium oxide therefore never forms. The heli-arc welder saved rods and eliminated the need to grind away the metal deposits formed in using the arc welder. Smith used his heli-arc to make cubes and the faster arc welder to join them.

Making the cubes also proved problematic. They tended to buckle no matter what Smith did. He tried drilling holes to release the heat and he tried reinforcing rods; still they buckled. He finally found a solution by leaving a small section of the cube—four to five inches—open and permitting the cube to cool overnight. The following day he had no further problem in welding it shut.[10] During the heating process, the chromium in the steel migrated toward the source of heat. Along the granular boundaries were carbides that were as much as 90 percent chromium, which left black lines along the edges of many cubes, as if they had been outlined. Smith eliminated these lines in later "Cubis" by using low-carbon welding rods. Eventually he found a better solution: having accepted the idea of precut shapes, he took the next logical step and also had the cubes fabricated by Ryerson. Smith's savings in labor and time more than offset the extra cost charged by the fabricator. During the course of the "Cubi" series, Smith had as many as forty to fifty cubes of various sizes in stock.

The use of prefabricated plates logically led to Smith's "think pieces," the stencils that replaced sketches for the flat stainless-steel pieces and "Cubis." The cardboard cutouts were made to the scale of the plates and cubes. The strong frontality of the stainless-steel sculptures was influenced to some degree by the stencils, particularly in the case of the "Cubis," which, according to Leon Pratt, were never assembled on the floor. The cardboard stencils thus generated these sculptures in the flat.

In 1957 Smith produced five sculptures in silver. He had first used silver for one of the 1939 *Medals for Dishonor* and again in 1941 for his "medallion pins." Smith fabricated his first silver sculpture in 1952 when Charles Withers, president of Towle Silversmiths, Newburyport, Massachusetts, commissioned eight contemporary sculptors to make works in silver.[11] The works were intended to revive interest in the beauty of silver as an art medium and would be shown, along with examples from various civilizations through the ages, in an exhibition entitled "Sculpture in Silver from Islands in Time." Henry Francis Taylor, then director of the Metropolitan Museum, recommended to Withers that Smith, as "the only sculptor in America with fire in his belly,"[12] be selected as one of the eight. Smith produced *Birthday,* a rather free-form work in a horizontal format. With its clawlike lines, *Birthday* looks backward in feeling to the late 1940s.

The silver sculptures of 1957 were evidently intended not only for their own sake but also as prototypes for the large-scale stainless steel works that Smith had begun to make in the same year.[13] Smith likely derived the idea of using a prototype from the process (which he employed in the early 1950s) of laying out materials on a flat surface in order to decide on a preferred arrangement, which allowed him to see anticipated sculptures tangibly rather than only in preliminary sketches.

Smith had found in silver an ingenious solution to a difficult problem he faced in working with stainless steel. As mentioned earlier, he could not cut stainless steel. It was also quite expensive compared with the mild steel he had been previously using. Before deciding what shapes he wanted from Ryerson Steel, Smith had to have some idea of what the sculpture would be like. Using silver as a model answered that question. It could be cut, shaped, and joined. Silver's gleaming surface resembled that of stainless. It was relatively low in cost. Unused silver need not be discarded: instead it can be "melted down" with the only loss being that in fabrication.

When Smith began working in a new direction—for example, when he began using stainless steel—he was usually cautious and preferred to let his instincts guide him. Since *The Hero* (Fig. 40) of 1951, he had been constructing anthropomorphic works with a pronounced central axis, a beginner's technique for creating balanced sculptures. *Voltri I* (Fig. 53), for example, is conceptually different from the following "Voltris": Smith took shapes similar to the cubes he had been using at Bolton Landing and merely stacked them one on top of another to produce an upright figure. Again, the silver sculpture *Lonesome Man* (1957; Fig. 72) reverts back to the central axis, topped by a square clipped on one corner to simulate a head in profile. By itself that arrangement would have been quite ordinary. The significance of this sculpture, however, lies in the second necklike form that swoops downward in a graceful diagonal direction. Here we find the beginning of the head-and-neck arrangements that would eventually lead, in the "Cubis," to an alternative to vertical formats.

The basic configuration of *Lonesome Man* was repeated the next year in *Fifteen Planes* (1958; Fig. 73), a large stainless-steel sculpture. Its major thematic elements sprawl on a tall vertical axis, with additional support from the diagonal. At first glance there seems to be no recognizable image in the splay of steel plates. The head-and-neck arrangement of *Lonesome Man* is present, however, even in the diagonal sweep and the jutting noselike sections in the lower quadrants. *Fifteen Planes* emphasizes the interplay of plates; the image has to be carefully sought. Another close parallel exists between the head-and-neck arrangement of the silver *Three Books and Apple* of 1957 and that of the large stainless-steel *Lectern Sentinel* of 1961. In both of those works the second neck is mounted horizontally above the usual vertical axis and the head is a circle perched on the end of the horizontal form. This pattern is repeated in the stainless-steel *Two Circle Sentinel* of 1961. In *Cubetotem 7 and 6* (1961; Fig. 74) the configuration consists primarily of verticals and horizontals. Attached to one of the two verticals, however, is another diagonal head-and-neck arrangement, which conflicts with the emphasis on abstraction in the rest of the piece. Smith had still not moved sufficiently far from the anthropomorphism of his diagonal forms. Adhering to the pattern, *Cubi XIV* (1963; Fig. 75) continues to reflect overdependence on a literally diagonal head and neck, which constrain spatial interplay. When only the sense of the diagonal is retained, it becomes an expressive force of considerable power, as in *Cubi VII* (1963; Fig. 76) (despite retention of its head), *Cubi IX* (1961; Fig. 77), and *Cubi XVI* (1963; Fig. 78).

All of the major works of the late 1950s employed flat plates. Smith had begun to use cubes in 1956, but the sculptures employing them are so rigidly vertical that the work appears academic. The use of cubes had been of interest to Smith since at least 1948 or 1949. Herman Cherry remembers watching while Smith, working on his house, began to place cement blocks one atop another. He later repeated the process with cardboard cartons.[14] The idea remained. In a 1952 sketchbook, recalling the work of the sixteenth-

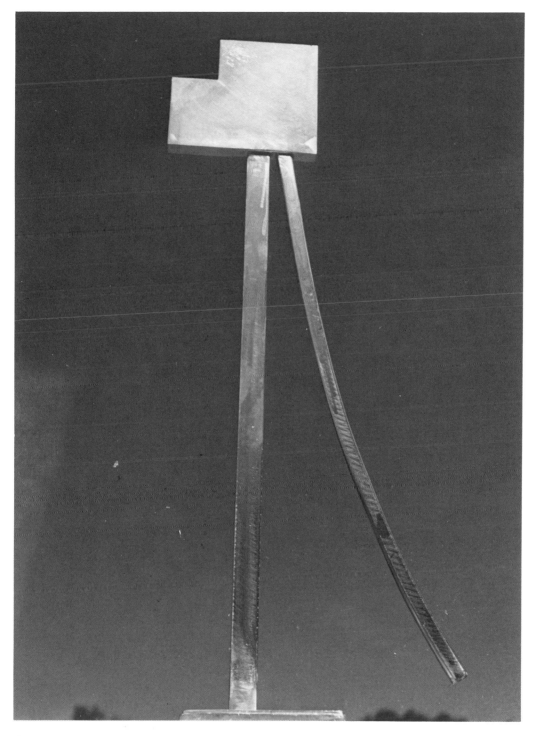

Fig. 72. *Lonesome Man,* 1957. Silver. 28 × 9 × 2″. Collection Candida and Rebecca Smith. Photo by David Smith

Fig. 73. *Fifteen Planes,* 1958. Stainless steel. 113¾ × 59 × 16″. Collection and photo courtesy The Seattle Art Museum. The Virginia Wright Fund, 74.1

166

Fig. 74. *Cubetotem 7 and 6,* 1961. Stainless steel. 123½ × 90½ × 22″. Collection Pepsico, Purchase, New York. Photo by David Smith

Fig. 75. *Cubi XIV*, 1963. Stainless steel. H. 121½″. Collection The St. Louis Art Museum. Photo by David Smith

168

Fig. 76. *Cubi VII*, 1963. Stainless steel. H. 111⅜″. Collection and photo courtesy The Art Institute of Chicago. Grant J. Pick Purchase Fund

Fig. 77. *Cubi IX,* 1961. Stainless steel. 106¼ × 56 × 46″. Collection and photo courtesy Walker Art Center, Minneapolis. Photo by Eric Sutherland

Fig. 78. *Cubi XVI,* 1963. Stainless steel. 132 × 60 × 33″. Collection Albright-Knox Art Gallery, Buffalo. Gift of The Seymour H. Knox Foundation, Inc., 1968. Photo courtesy Marlborough-Gerson Gallery, Inc., New York

century Mannerist painter Luca Cambiaso, Smith wrote: "The idea of volumes by reducing the human form to cubes—exploited by Cambiaso"[15] (Fig. 79).

Both Clement Greenberg and Stephen Weil, who was then Smith's representative at Marlborough-Gerson, saw *Cubetotem 7 and 6* as a transitional work between the flat, stainless sculptures and the "Cubis."[16] Found in a Bronx warehouse after Smith's death, it has two sets of verticals joined at the bottom by a spread of horizontal, flattened cubes. The vertical columns strongly suggest the anthropomorphic images that had been typical of Smith's work; the right vertical contains the familiar head-and-neck arrangement and a flattened cube in place of Smith's frequently used picture-plane torso.

Smith's use of flattened cubes in place of plates was apparently an effort to introduce depth. The frontal plane is, however, still there. Despite the two totemic themes, the strong horizontal line at the bottom of *Cubetotem 7 and 6* recalls the picture frames of the early 1950s. Even the head and neck, despite their diagonal position, suggest a partially closed upper side to the frame. It is an uncharacteristically ambiguous work: the "Cubis" generally have either strongly anthropomorphic images and a strong vertical line or "picture frames" that emphasize the horizontal (Fig. 80, c. 1965). The double totemic theme may have been unprecedented in Smith's oeuvre. The addition of a strong horizontal thrust has created within this single work the sense of the two major themes of the "Cubi" series.

When Smith first investigated an idea, he was, as we have seen, frequently quite cautious, resorting to the figure for his point of departure. When he approached the early "Cubis," it was perhaps the awareness that he was introducing a major series and, as well, the requirements of the images themselves which held him back from the kind of expression we see in the later and more pictorial "Cubis." Whatever the reason, in such examples as *Cubi II, Cubi III* (1961; Fig. 81), and *Cubi VI,* weakness results from the compromises made between the image and the exigencies of modular construction. In neither *Cubi III* nor *Cubi VI* do we sense the powerful presence associated with Smith's totemic forms. Nor are the needs of modular construction well served. The forms are densely packed and have little to do with space. Interestingly, of the three, *Cubi II* is the most satisfactory. Smith developed his totemic form freely, making no effort to involve space.

With *Cubi VIII* Smith began to pull away from anthropomorphism. *Cubi IX* (Fig. 77) shows only slight ambiguity in totemic and pictorial ideas. Here we see again the double totemic images of *Cubetotem 7 and 6*, though *Cubi IX* projects much farther into depth. On the right side are both diagonal and horizontal necks. The absence of heads relieves this work of its burden of anthropomorphism, however, and allows Smith to perch the modules in such a way that they encroach on the space between the verticals. The elements are so delicately balanced on edges and the vertical columns so disjointed that the simple totemic origins of *Cubi IX* are obscured. The middle "Cubis," including *Cubi XI* and *Cubi XII* (1963; Fig. 82), continue to reflect the ambiguity in the anthropomorphic figure and the pictorial image represented by the picture frame. In *Cubi XII,* the picture-plane torso has been so expanded that it almost but not quite takes over the vertical column. If we look again at *The Hero* (Fig. 40), we can see that, despite the complexities Smith has introduced since 1951, the origins of *Cubi XII* are still clear.

Fig. 79. Luca Cambiaso. "Group of Cubist Figures," late 16th century. Drawing on paper. Dimensions unknown. Collection Gabinetto Disegni e Stampe degli Uffizi, Florence. Photo courtesy Scala/Editorial Photocolor Archives

173

Fig. 80. "Cubis" in fields at Bolton Landing, c. 1965. Photo by David Smith

174

Fig. 81. *Cubi III,* 1961. Stainless steel. 95½ × 33¼ × 19¼″. Collection Beatrice and Philip Gersh, Beverly Hills, California. Photo courtesy Marlborough-Gerson Gallery, Inc., New York

175

Fig. 82. *Cubi XII,* 1963. Stainless steel. 109⅝ × 49¼ × 32¼″. Collection and photo courtesy Hirshhorn Museum and Sculpture Garden, Smithsonian Institution, Washington, D.C.

Fig. 83. *Cubi XVII*, 1963. Stainless steel. 107¾ × 64⅞ × 38⅛″. Collection and photo courtesy Dallas Museum of Fine Arts. The Eugene and Margaret McDermott Fund

Cubi XVII (1963; Fig. 83), *Cubi XVIII* (1964; Fig. 84), *Cubi XIX* (1964; Fig. 85), and *Cubi XX* (1964; Fig. 86) are the key sculptures in the development of a new use for the picture frame. Here Smith departed from his customary pattern of using frames to define frontal planes. Now the frames rise in jagged pieces and occupy deep space. Note the platforms, which in Smith's work always signify the absence of frontality. Having lost their functional purpose, the frames became points of departure for inventiveness in the use of modules. *Cubi XVII* contains the most recognizable frame of the four. All sides of the picture frame are present, twisted only slightly from the frontal plane. In *Cubi XVIII* we see a collapsing frame mounted on three cubes. *Cubi XIX* carries the collapsing-frame idea to a later stage of collapse by allowing several sides to ''fall'' directly on the platform. In this last work of the series, two of the four sides have been turned into cubes. In an almost playful aside, Smith changed the position of the seat from the top of the base column where it appears in *Cubi XVIII* to the platform along with the other forms. In *Cubi XX*, however, Smith returned to the pattern of four sides rising from the platform.

Cubi XXIII (1964; Fig. 87) has frequently been interpreted as an anthropomorphic image, as a kind of ''walking man'' metaphor. From the preceding discussion, we should know that such interpretations are incorrect. They overlook the fact that rarely are the late ''Cubis'' anthropomorphic and that they almost all show a consistent thematic concern with the use of the picture frame. In *Cubi XXIII* the frame has been split into two segments. This sculpture heralds a return to a focus on the frame and reestablishes the frontal mode. When it is viewed in this light, the cylinder to the left is understandable as the familiar pedestal, now divested of its platform—a loss consistent with the revitalization of frontality. Smith showed striking inventiveness in placing the frame on the ground, adjacent to rather than atop the pedestal. Relieved of its functional purpose, the support becomes purely a sculptural component and the pedestal as such is eliminated.

With *Cubi XXIV* (1964; Fig. 88), *Cubi XXVII* (1965; Fig. 89), and *Cubi XXVIII* (1965; Fig. 90), the three so-called ''Gate'' pieces, Smith returned to intact frames and clearly defined frontal planes. The frames are strangely vacant. With no subjects within their borders, the frames themselves become the areas of interest.

In the ''Gate'' works, Smith again demonstrated a facility for giving aesthetic emphasis to elements that might otherwise be considered functional. His focus on the frame recalls his trip to Europe in 1935, when Smith's attention to the paintings of the old masters was distracted by the condition of the frames and the cracks in the paint.

We may be stretching a point to see the columns of the ''Gate'' pieces as a continuation of the double totems, but at the very least the earlier work taught Smith to value the imagistic potential in the vertical members of the frame and to use them ingeniously. The power of *Cubi XXVII* in particular is derived from its verticals. The delicately balanced modular columns have a grace that reminds us of those in *Cubi IX* (Fig. 77). By his sensitive linking of massive forms he again demonstrated mastery in using the unique strength of welded joints to create expressive modes. The artfully created tensions, which he achieved by setting modules on implausible edges, are derived from his experiments with balanced forms in the ''Cubi'' sculptures. In such works as *Cubi XIII, Cubi XXI,* and

Fig. 84. *Cubi XVIII,* 1964. Stainless steel. 115¾ × 60 × 21¾″. Collection and photo courtesy Museum of Fine Arts, Boston. Gift of Stephen D. Paine

Fig. 85. *Cubi XIX,* 1964. Stainless steel. 113⅛ × 21¾ × 20¾″. Collection and photo courtesy
The Tate Gallery, London

Fig. 86. *Cubi XX,* 1964. Stainless steel. 111 × 55 × 56½″. Collection University of California at Los Angeles. Gift of David E. Bright. Photo by Frank Thomas

Fig. 87. *Cubi XXIII*, 1964. Stainless steel. 76¼ × 172⅞ × 26¾". Collection and photo courtesy Los Angeles County Museum of Art. Contemporary Art Council Fund

182

Fig. 88. *Cubi XXIV,* 1964. Stainless steel. 114¼ × 84¼ × 32″. Collection Museum of Art, Carnegie Institute, Pittsburgh. Howard Heinz Endowment Purchase Fund, 1967. Photo by David Smith

183

Fig. 89. *Cubi XXVII*, 1965. Stainless steel. 111⅜ × 87¾ × 34″. Collection and photo courtesy The Solomon R. Guggenheim Museum, New York. Photo by Robert E. Mates

184

Fig. 90. *Cubi XXVIII,* 1965. Stainless steel. 108 × 112 × 40″. Collection and photo courtesy Norton Simon, Inc. Museum of Art, Pasadena

Fig. 91. *Cubi XXV,* 1965. Stainless steel. Dimensions unknown. Whereabouts unknown. Photo by David Smith

186

Cubi XXV (1965: Fig. 91) the handling of balance is almost pedestrian, as if Smith had been considering a new direction but turned cautious.

Though in the "Cubi" pieces the flatness associated with Smith's work is combined with three-dimensional modular forms, the two sculptures that might sum up his lifetime of work are essentially flat. These works, *Becca* (1965; Fig. 92) and *Untitled (Candida)* (1965; Fig. 93), epitomize the two directions in which Smith had traveled since 1950. *Becca* recapitulates both the problems and the strengths in Smith's use of anthropomorphic figures. The tension between the diagonals and the horizontal interlocking plates is only partially resolved. The sheer raw power of the upright image, however, presses the demand to see it as a figure, even over the massive horizontal plates. The monstrous form, looking like some giant pagan idol, arrests the spectator's eye and forces a confrontation. Its strength exists because Smith avoided the mistake he made in his anthropomorphic "Cubis." In such works as *Cubi III* and *Cubi VI* he tried to translate too literally his modular cubes into figures. The resulting cleverness—one might even say cuteness—robs those works of the image-making qualities found in the best of Smith's anthropomorphic sculptures. In *Becca* Smith came to use modular forms that must have satisfied even his lust for bigness.

Untitled (Candida)'s steel plates, though also impressively large, are not as large as those of *Becca*. The warpage created by the heat of a welding torch, which gives one of *Becca's* massive upper plates its idiosyncratic appearance, is missing here. The reduced scale of the plates in *Untitled (Candida)* renders them both visually and technically more modular than those of *Becca*. As in the "Gate" series, the center is left open so that attention is focused on the subject, the frame. *Untitled (Candida)* lacks the delicately perched forms we see in *Cubi XXVII*. Instead, there are only overlapping steel plates, arranged in such a way that the work comes out as among the most ascetic that Smith produced. It fulfills a vision of twenty years earlier:

> Extreme subtleties of form indicated by very small differences in distance quotients. Structurally the difference of 1/16" in thickness has a great deal to do with function. When I superimpose three varying thicknesses of metal upon each other that indicates form levels though these may play a small part in an object assembly which for certain reasons I want to appear as a profile bas relief.[17]

Untitled (Candida) indicates Smith's second direction. Its frame is symbolic of the many other pictorial works he made. One of their chief characteristics is that they are usually horizontal in format. By contrast, the anthropomorphic works are primarily vertical. But toward the end, Smith's work had become horizontal. *Becca* is a hybrid that creates considerable tension through its impulses in both directions.

Becca and *Untitled (Candida)* offer a summary of the ideas that had always been in Smith's oeuvre. His images seldom changed. What did change was the way in which they were presented. Smith's interest in frames can be seen in his reactions in the mid-1930s to European art. Platforms had captured his attention when as a student painter he piled paint

Fig. 92. *Becca,* 1965. Stainless steel. 113½ × 120½ × 30″. Collection and photo courtesy The Metropolitan Museum of Art. Bequest of Adelaide Milton de Groot (1876–1967), Exchange, 1972

Fig. 93. *Untitled (Candida)*, 1965. Stainless steel. 101 × 119¾ × 30¾″. Collection Candida and Rebecca Smith. Photo by David Smith

and other materials "so high that a base was required where the canvas should be."[18] Success came when he learned how to combine his images with the kind of medium that was essential to him both as a person and as an artist. Though he learned slowly, he learned well. Starting in 1950, he focused on just a few images, varying them in so many ingenious ways that he created an impression of eclecticism. By the end of his career, just a few images were sufficient. They could be manipulated in countless ways. Coming when they do, *Becca* and *Untitled (Candida)* raise at least one important question. Smith had progressed from the flat stainless-steel sculptures of the late 1950s through the platformed "Cubis" and ultimately to modification of the frontal plane in the "Gate" series, with its limited depth. Was the flatness of *Becca* and *Untitled (Candida)* a return to the ideas of the late 1950s, or did it signal a new direction?

Smith died at the height of his creative power. On May 23, 1965, on his way from a visit to Kenneth Noland in Shaftsbury, Vermont, he drove off the road; his carry-all truck turned over and Smith died. Having achieved the recognition he had sought for so long, he was not able to savor it. Those who had known him best had recognized an unbreachable isolation. In 1951 Smith wrote, "I sit up here and dream of the city as I used to dream of the mountains when I sat on the dock in Brooklyn."[19] Though Bolton Landing came close, no place was truly home to that lonely spirit.

NOTES

CHAPTER 1

1. David Smith file, reel 2, frame 941, n.d., Archives of American Art, Smithsonian Institution, Washington, D.C. (hereafter cited as AAA).

CHAPTER 2

1. Smith file, reel 4, frame 1082, 1961, AAA.

2. In his two semesters at Ohio University, of six grades in other than art courses, Smith received two F's, two D-minuses, and two D's; at best he would have been on probation. Ibid., reel 1, frame 004, n.d.

3. Ibid., reel 4, frame 360, 1952.

4. Ibid., frame 387, 1953.

5. Sources of information on Smith's life before his arrival in New York are limited. The best source is Dorothy Dehner, his first wife, to whom he was married for twenty five years. Dehner was very close to her mother-in-law and remained so long after her divorce from Smith. Other sources include Jean Freas Pond, Smith's second wife and the mother of Rebecca and Candida, their two children; Smith's own writings; and of course the Archives of American Art, which is the main source of information on Smith after his arrival in New York.

6. Smith file, reel 4, frames 1097–99, n.d., AAA.

7. Interview with Dorothy Dehner, December 1975.

8. Ibid.

9. Dorothy Dehner attested to Graham's statement regarding Smith, and Smith attested to the statement about de Kooning. Dorothy Dehner, Foreword, and Marcia Allentuck, Introduction, in *John Graham's System and Dialectics of Art,* ed. Marcia Allentuck (Baltimore: Johns Hopkins University Press, 1971), pp. xiv, 15.

10. Ibid.

11. Lee Krasner, Pollock's widow, told Dorothy Dehner of a conversation during which Graham told her that anyone who became successful could no longer be his friend. Dehner interview.

12. Smith file, reel 4, frame 1093, n.d., AAA.

13. Dorothy Dehner to James Brehm, November 18, 1972, in Dehner file, reel 796, frame 235, AAA.

NOTES

14. David Smith to Edgar Levy, September 6, 1933, in Lucille Corcos Levy file, frame 0048, AAA.

15. Sketchbooks 1–4, 1936–38, Smith file, reel 3, AAA.

16. Smith file, reel 4, frame 389, 1953.

17. George Biddle file, reel P-17, frames 772 and 774, AAA.

18. Cleve Gray, ed., *David Smith by David Smith* (New York: Holt, Rinehart & Winston, 1968), p. 27; and Dehner interview.

19. Dehner interview.

CHAPTER 3

1. Garnett McCoy, ed., *David Smith* (New York: Praeger, 1973), p. 172.

2. In the 1929 issue of *Cahiers d'art* there appeared two articles on Picasso. The first, "Picasso à Dinard, été 1928" by Christian Zervos, included a photograph of *Project for a Sculpture in Iron Wire,* which was the one Smith had to have seen. In the article Zervos describes how he saw Picasso pick up a wire and twist it while speaking until, in a few minutes, it underwent great changes in sensibility. Smith could not read French, but John Graham, who brought back issues of *Cahiers d'art* from France for the Smiths, may have translated the article. Thus Smith, who almost surely was influenced by his memory of the photograph when he made his "drawings in air" in 1950 and 1951, may have also been influenced by the article's description of how Picasso could improvise in three dimensions.

In "Projects de Picasso pour un monument," the second article, there is no reference to welded sculpture (or of Julio Gonzalez, who had done the welding for Picasso), but there is one to iron wire ("fil de fer"). Later, Smith, writing an article on Gonzalez, did not refer to Picasso's welded sculptures, which they were, but spoke of "iron" ones—additional evidence that he may have had both articles translated for him.

3. Dehner interview.

4. L. C. Levy file, frame 0075, c. 1935, AAA.

5. Ibid., frames 0019–21, c. 1935.

6. Smith file, reel 4, frame 357, 1952, AAA.

7. L. C. Levy file, frame 0029, c. 1935, AAA.

8. In the 1975 interview Dorothy Dehner insisted that it was Gonzalez's work in *Cahiers d'art,* not Picasso's, that had so aroused Smith's excitement. She described the issue's cover as being blue and white, and the Gonzalez feature as having photographs across the top of the page and text beneath. The first issue of *Cahiers d'art* to feature Gonzalez's work appeared in 1935 and was the only one with a blue-and-white cover. The same issue included photos of works by Jacques Lipchitz and Alberto Giacometti, two artists who greatly influenced Smith's work during the late 1930s. The issue was indeed a rich one for sculptors interested in avant-garde art.

9. Smith file, reel 4, frame 359, 1952, AAA.

10. Edgar Levy file, frame 294, 1948, AAA.

11. Dehner interview.

12. Sketchbook 15, c. 1941, in Smith file, reel 3, frame 688, AAA.

13. As Jane Harrison Cone pointed out on page 7 of her introduction to the catalogue for the "David Smith 1906–1965" retrospective exhibition at the Fogg Art Museum, Cambridge, Mass.,

September 28–November 15, 1966, Smith probably saw the Giacometti work at the Modern's "Fantastic Art, Dada, Surrealism" exhibition, December 9, 1936–January 17, 1937.

14. Edward Fry, *David Smith,* exhibition catalogue (New York: Solomon R. Guggenheim Museum, 1969), p. 41.

15. This phrase was coined by Clement Greenberg to describe Smith's linear structures of the early 1950s.

CHAPTER 4

1. David Smith, "Memories to Myself," Archives of American Art Quarterly *Journal* 8, no. 2 (April 1968):11.

2. Smith file, reel 1, frame 293, 1942, AAA.

3. Dehner interview. Though Dehner recalls Harari as the person who recommended Smith to Marian Willard, she thinks Julien Levy may also have done so. Willard remembers only Levy.

4. Smith to Willard, August 28, 1942, in Marian Willard file, reel 986, no frame no., AAA.

5. Sketchbook 7, c. 1939, Smith file, reel 3, frame 524, AAA.

6. David Smith, "Modern Sculpture and Society," in McCoy, ed., *David Smith,* p. 42.

7. Rosalind Krauss, *Terminal Iron Works* (Cambridge, Mass.: MIT Press, 1971), p. 35n.

8. David Smith, "Perception and Reality," in McCoy, ed., *David Smith,* p. 78.

9. Emily Genauer, *New York Herald Tribune,* February 21, 1960, reproduced in Smith file, reel 5, frame 821, AAA.

10. Smith file, reel 4, frame 361, 1952.

11. As quoted in Emily Genauer, review of Smith's 1957 exhibition at the Museum of Modern Art, reproduced in ibid., reel 5, frame 818.

12. Willard to Katherine Kuh, February 6, 1941, in Willard file, reel 986, no frame no., AAA.

13. Elizabeth McCausland, *Springfield [Mass.] Union and Republican,* November 10, 1940, reproduced in Smith file, reel 4, frame 594. This article provided most of my information on Smith's attitudes and techniques in making the *Medals for Dishonor.* Another article, on Smith's techniques, appeared in the same newspaper on March 3, 1940. For information on the background of the *Medals,* see Dorothy Dehner, "Medals for Dishonor: The Fifteen Medallions of David Smith," *Art Journal* 37 (Winter 1977–78):144–50.

14. Smith to Willard, December 16, 1941, in Willard file, reel 986, no frame no., AAA.

15. Smith to Willard, April 21, 1942, in ibid.

16. Smith to J. D. Hatch, n.d., in Smith file, reel 1, frames 271–74, AAA.

17. Smith to War Production Board, May 30, 1942, in ibid., frame 280.

CHAPTER 5

1. Clement Greenberg, "American Sculpture of Our Time: Group Show," *Nation* 156, no. 4 (January 23, 1943):140–41.

2. Milton Brown, "After Three Years," *Magazine of Art* 39 (April 1946): 138.

3. Robert Cronbach, reproduced in Smith file, reel 5, frame 764, AAA.

4. *Time* 35, no. 17 (April 22, 1940): 70.

NOTES

5. Maude Riley, "Sewer Pipe Sculpture," *Cue*, March 16, 1940; reproduced in Smith file, reel 5, frame 599, AAA.

6. Interview with the late Thomas Hess, February 1976.

7. Interview with Herman Cherry, February 11, 1976.

8. First draft of Woodstock conference speech, 1952, in Smith file, reel 4, frame 368, AAA.

9. Willard to Smith, May 22, 1943, in Willard file, reel 986, no frame no., AAA.

10. Hess interview. It is not difficult to understand Barr's dilemma. American artists were clamoring and picketing against the European bias of the Museum of Modern Art during the 1930s. Yet the European avant-grade—Jacques Lipchitz, Joaquin Torres-Garcia, Pablo Gargallo, Julio Gonzalez, Alberto Giacometti—were working in a wide range of styles and ideas, while the Americans were limiting themselves to smoothly biomorphic forms that led straight back to Brancusi. Smith and Lassaw were the only exceptions.

11. Smith to Willard, February 1, 1956, in Willard file, reel 986, frame 693, AAA.

12. Willard to Smith, May 22, 1943, in Smith file, reel 1, frame 313, AAA.

13. Smith to Museum of Modern Art, July 14, 1944, in ibid., frame 342.

14. Smith to Willard, September 22, 1940, in Willard file, reel 986, no frame no., AAA.

15. Smith to Willard, May 1943, in ibid.

16. Smith to Willard, July 24, 1944, in ibid.

17. Willard to Smith, March 28, 1942, in Smith file, reel 1, frame 266, AAA.

18. Rosalind Krauss, "The Sculpture of David Smith" (Ph.D. dissertation, Harvard University, 1969):190.

19. Fry, *David Smith*, p. 11.

20. Smith to Willard, n.d., in Willard file, reel 986, no frame no., AAA.

CHAPTER 6

1. Dorothy Dehner to Edgar Levy, September 29, 1944, in Edgar Levy file, frame 244, AAA.

2. October 1946, in ibid., frame 272.

3. David Smith to Levy, March 27, 1947, in ibid., frame 276.

4. The information on this period of Smith's life, available in the Edgar Levy and Marian Willard files at the AAA, has been supplemented by interviews with Dorothy Dehner.

5. Dorothy Dehner to Levy, September 15, 1948, in E. Levy file, no frame no., AAA.

6. David Smith to Dorothy Dehner, n.d.; letter in possession of Dorothy Dehner.

7. Telephone interview with Dorothy Dehner, January 25, 1983.

8. Interview with Jean Freas Pond, December 5, 1975.

9. Smith file, reel 1, frames 1131, 1226, 1246, 1247, AAA.

10. Smith to Willard, January 31, 1947, in Willard file, reel 986, no frame no., AAA.

11. Smith to Willard, May 14, 1948, in ibid.

12. Sidney Geist, "Prelude: The 1930s," *Arts* 30 (September 1956):49–55; reproduced in Smith file, reel 5, frames 703–6, AAA.

13. Herman Cherry to David Smith, August 6, 1947, in ibid., reel 1, frame 573.

14. David Smith, "The Sculptor's Relationship to the Museum, Dealer, and Public," in McCoy, ed., *David Smith*, p. 52.

15. Smith file, reel 4, frames 300–10, AAA.

16. Ibid.

17. Smith to Cherry, October 12, 1947, in ibid., reel 1, frame 587.

18. Smith to Juliana Force, November 8, 1947, in ibid., frame 601.

19. Smith to Hudson Walker, November 8, 1947, in ibid., frame 600.

20. Smith to Walker, January 3, 1948, in ibid., frame 623.

CHAPTER 7

1. See the "Aunt Flo" letters, Figs. 2, 3, and 4.

2. Smith file, reel 1, frame 957, AAA.

3. Ibid., frame 954

4. Ibid., frames 933, 957. (Smith tended to understate sales. The figure seems impossibly low for an artist then considered by important critics as the best sculptor in the U.S.)

5. Willard to Smith, n.d., in ibid., reel 3, frame 218.

6. Willard to Smith, December 5, 1946, in ibid. reel 1, frame 444.

7. Robert Beverly Hale, *Metropolitan Museum of Art Bulletin* 8, no. 5 (January 1950):135

8. Theodore Roszak to Smith, n.d., in Smith file, reel 3, frame 381, AAA.

9. Smith to Roszak, n.d., in ibid., frame 381.

10. Smith speech to the Metropolitan Art Association, January 23, 1952, in ibid., reel 4, frame 351.

11. Thomas Hess to Smith, July 15, 1953, in ibid., reel 1, frame 1277.

12. Interview with Dorothy Miller, January 1976.

13. Smith to Miller, October 6, 1953, in Smith file, reel 1, frame 1314, AAA.

14. Ibid., frame 1307.

15. Alfred Barr to Smith, November 24, 1953, in ibid., frame 1329.

16. Smith to Barr, December 1, 1953, in ibid., frame 1331.

17. Ibid.

18. James Thrall Soby to Smith, December 12, 1957, in ibid., reel 2, frame 439.

19. Alfred Barr to Smith, October 17, 1957, in ibid., frame 408.

20. George Rickey to Smith, March 25, 1954, in ibid., reel 1, frame 1399.

21. Smith to G. David Thompson, July 11, 1955, in ibid., reel 2, frame 197.

22. Herman Cherry to Smith, date listed as 1956 (may be inaccurate), in ibid., frame 334.

23. Smith to Willard, January 28, 1956, in Willard file, reel 986, frame 687, AAA.

24. Smith to Dan Johnson (Marian Willard's husband), n.d., in ibid., frame 694.

25. Smith to Corcoran Gallery, October 30, 1956, in Smith file, reel 2, frame 322, AAA.

26. Interviews with Marian Willard, October 1975 and January 1976.

27. Herman Cherry to Smith, n.d., in Smith file, reel 2, frame 334.

CHAPTER 8

1. Herman Cherry kindly permitted me to extract his letter to Smith, which is reproduced in Smith file, reel 1, frame 1044, AAA.

2. According to Smith's account, he acquired the letter forms when he bought up the stock of an old wagon-and-buggy shop (Smith to Dorothy Miller, March 8, 1957, David Smith file, Museum of

Modern Art Collection: Painting and Sculpture, New York). This account conflicts with Dorothy Dehner's recollection that she discovered the letter forms in a hardware store and called them to Smith's attention. Dehner even recalled the name of the store, Finch-Pryers. This appears to be an instance in which Smith romanticized a prosaic incident. Dehner's account seems the more accurate, especially as Finch-Pryers was a store the Smiths often visited. Dehner interview December 1975.

    3. Pond interview.

    4. Smith wrote of *24 Greek Y's:* "In these sculptures, I have sought object identity by symbols, demanding the return to symbol origin, *before these purities were befouled by words*" (emphasis added). He betrays some inconsistency, however, when he then says that *Y* is the symbol for the word "why," thus connecting *24 Greek Y's* with the visual puns of *The Banquet* and *The Letter.* Smith file, February 27, 1951, reel 1, frame 955, AAA.

    5. Krauss, "Sculpture of David Smith": 252.

    6. Dehner interview, December 1975.

    7. Smith to Willard, March 2, 1942, in Willard file, reel 986, no frame no.

    8. Smith to Dr. Bayerthal, July 30, 1961, in Smith file, reel 2, frame 913.

    9. Clement Greenberg, personal communication, March 25, 1978.

CHAPTER 9

    1. Unsorted papers of David Smith, AAA.

    2. W. R. Valentiner, "Sculpture by David Smith," *Arts and Architecture* 65, no. 8 (August 1948): 22–23, 51.

    3. Speech delivered on radio station WNYC, New York, December 30, 1952, in Smith file, reel 4, frame 363, AAA.

    4. Elaine de Kooning, "David Smith Makes a Sculpture," *Art News* 50, no. 5 (September 1951): 38–41, 50–51.

    5. Speech delivered in Portland, Ore., March 23, 1953, in Smith file, reel 4, frame 387.

    6. Speech delivered at Newcomb College, New Orleans, March 21, 1951, in ibid., frame 451.

    7. Unsorted papers of David Smith, AAA.

    8. Hilton Kramer, "David Smith: Stencils for Sculpture," *Art in America* 50, no. 4 (Winter 1962):32–43.

    9. Smith's use of found objects in an aesthetic context differs, of course, from the way they were earlier used by Marcel Duchamp.

    10. Smith had been inspired by the way Gonzalez's forms moved through space. In this instance Smith read more into the idea than was there to be seen: Gonzalez's forms were still much related to the object. They were sufficiently fluid, however, to enable Smith to sense how effectively space could be used.

    11. Notes for de Kooning article (see n. 4 above), in Smith file, reel 4, frames 490–500, AAA.

    12. Smith to Greenberg, January 6, 1953, in ibid., reel 1, frame 1213.

    13. Notes for de Kooning article (see n. 4 above), in ibid., reel 4, frames 490–500.

    14. Inventory, Estate of David Smith, on file with Ira Lowe, Attorney at Law and estate executor, Washington, D.C.

    15. Unsorted papers of David Smith, AAA.

    16. McCoy, ed., *David Smith,* p. 173.

17. Interview with the late Leon Pratt, July 1970.

18. Smith to Margaret McKellar, Whitney Museum, October 30, 1956, in Smith file, reel 2, frame 321, AAA.

19. Smith complained that he sold only one work in 1950, and that for less than $340 (Smith to Emily Genauer, February 26, 1951, in ibid., reel 1, frame 953). An undated notation by Smith indicates that the only piece sold during 1950–51, *Billiard Player,* was bought by Roy Newberger for $333 (ibid., frame 956). Yet on August 19, 1951, George Schloss wrote to Smith in regard to *24 Greek Y's,* which he had purchased (ibid., frame 1016). This work was made in 1950 and consequently must have been sold during the 1950–51 period. In addition, the Munson-Williams-Proctor Institute, Utica, N.Y., wrote Smith on May 24, 1951, for information about *The Letter,* made in 1950, which it had purchased (ibid., frame 987). Thus Smith failed to note at least two sales that must have been made in either 1950 or 1951.

20. Smith to Willard, October 9, 1950, in Willard file, reel 986, frame 547, AAA.

21. Smith to Willard, September 3, 1954, in ibid., frame 642.

22. Smith to Willard, December 7, 1954, in ibid., frame 657.

23. Smith to Willard, January 31, 1947, in ibid., no frame no.

24. Smith file, reel 2, frame 455, AAA.

25. Dan Johnson to Lloyd Goodrich, October 24, 1957, in David Smith file, Whitney Museum, New York.

CHAPTER 10

1. Interview with the late Andrew Ritchie, 1976.

2. Ibid.

3. Sam Hunter to Smith, n.d., in Smith file, reel 2, frame 566, AAA.

4. Herman Cherry to Smith, August 15, 1957, in ibid., frame 380.

5. Cherry interview.

6. Pond interview.

7. Sketchbook 15, c. 1941, in Smith file, reel 3, frame 688, AAA.

8. Sketchbook 40, 1950–54, in ibid., frame 1306.

9. Clement Greenberg, Personal communication, May 24, 1979.

10. Otto Gerson to Smith, August 22, 1960, in Smith file, reel 2, frame 795, AAA.

11. Smith to Gerson, July 30, 1961, in ibid., frame 912.

12. *Cello Player* was sent on approval to Lois Orswell for $4,050 net (after a 10 percent discount), on January 15, 1958, in ibid., frame 467.

13. Undated and unaddressed memorandum signed "L.G." (obviously Lloyd Goodrich) documenting a telephone conversation with Smith on July 8, 1958, in Sara Roby Foundation file, American Federation of Arts, New York.

14. Smith to Goodrich, August 15, 1958, in ibid.

15. Goodrich to Walter G. Dunnington, Jr., Attorney at Law, March 19, 1959, in ibid.

16. Smith to Goodrich, April 4 or 6, 1959, in ibid.

17. Smith to Marian Willard, October 9, 1950, in Smith file, reel 1, frame 848, AAA.

18. Ken Sawyer to Smith, April 19, 1960, in ibid., reel 2, frames 749 and 750; and Greenberg, personal communication, March 20, 1979.

19. Hess interview.

20. Smith to Leo Castelli, August 1, 1960, in Smith file, reel 2, frame 783, AAA.

21. Castelli to Smith, August 2, 1960, in ibid., frame 784.

22. Smith to Castelli, August 7, 1960, in ibid., frame 785.

23. Castelli to Smith, August 11, 1960, in ibid., frame 786.

24. Gordon Washburn to Smith, October 21, 1960, in David Smith file, Museum of Art, Carnegie Institute, Pittsburgh.

25. Smith to Washburn, November 3, 1960, in ibid.

26. Leon Arkus to Smith, March 1, 1961, in ibid.

27. In response to Smith's request, Ellin found out that Carnegie charged 10 percent on all sales at the International. Everett Ellin to Smith, June 15, 1961, in Ellin file, reel N 738, frame 0043, AAA.

28. Smith to Otto Gerson, July 30, 1961, in Smith file, reel 2, frame 912, AAA.

29. Smith to Ellin, August 28, 1961, in Ellin file, reel N 738, frame 0038, AAA.

30. Arkus to Smith, August 30, 1961, in Smith file, Museum of Art, Carnegie Institute, Pittsburgh.

31. Smith to Arkus, September 5, 1961, in ibid.

32. Smith to Arkus, September 28, 1961, in ibid.

33. Arkus to Smith, October 10, 1961, in ibid.

34. Gordon Washburn to Smith, October 24, 1961, in ibid.

35. Arkus, personal communication, February 5, 1976.

36. Ibid.

37. James Truitt, personal communication, November 7, 1961. The "3d class virtue" refers to an incident cited in Smith's letter of rejection to the Carnegie Institute. (The letter is published in Gray, ed., *David Smith by David Smith,* p. 40.) In defending the prize system, Henry Francis Taylor, then director of the Metropolitan Museum, had referred to an ancient Roman custom of giving a prize for virginity; a painter then inquired about the technical requirements for second and third prizes.

38. Washburn to Smith, December 7, 1961, in Smith file, Museum of Art, Carnegie Institute, Pittsburgh.

39. Arkus to Smith, April 3, 1961, in ibid.

40. Cherry interview.

41. Miller interview.

42. Information regarding his divorce comes from interview with Jean Freas Pond, October 31, 1975.

43. Voucher stub from Universal Building North, Washington, D.C., and Smith to Jean Freas Smith, both in Smith file, reel 3, frames 0032 and 0037, AAA.

44. The majority of material regarding the West coast came from Ellin file, reel N 738, AAA, and was supplemented by Smith file, AAA.

45. Smith to Gerson, July 31, 1962, in Smith file, reel 2, frame 1074, AAA.

CHAPTER 11

1. During the July 1970 interview Leon Pratt described the task of holding the heavy platform on its point as being among the most difficult he had to perform for Smith.

2. Writings about Voltri, n.d., in Smith file, reel 4, frame 706, AAA.

3. Photographs of *Wagon I* and *Wagon II* inadvertently were reversed in Rosalind Krauss's *Sculpture of David Smith: A Catalogue Raisonné* (New York: Garland, 1977).

4. Pratt interview.

5. Clement Greenberg, personal communication, May 21, 1978.

6. Sketchbook 40, 1950–54, in Smith file, reel 3, frame 1338, AAA.

7. Pratt interview.

8. Smith to Greenberg, March 31, 1964, in Clement Greenberg file, reel N 737, frame 165, AAA.

9. Pratt interview.

10. Ibid.

11. Unsorted papers of David Smith, AAA.

12. Charles Withers, personal communication, May 22, 1971.

13. Smith to G. David Thompson, October 31, 1955, in Smith file, reel 2, frame 231, AAA.

14. Cherry interview.

15. Sketchbook 36, 1952, in Smith file, reel 3, frame 1174, AAA.

16. Interview with Stephen Weil, January 1976.

17. Sketchbook 24, 1946, in Smith file, reel 3, frame 936, AAA.

18. Undated writings, in ibid., reel 4, frame 1093

19. Notes for de Kooning article (see above Chap. 9, n. 4), in ibid., reel 4, frame 498.

SELECTED BIBLIOGRAPHY

PUBLICATIONS ON DAVID SMITH

Allentuck, Marcia, ed. *John Graham's System and Dialectics of Art*. Baltimore: Johns Hopkins University Press, 1970.

Ashton, Dore. *The New York School: A Cultural Reckoning*. New York: Viking, 1973.

Blake, William, and Christina Stead. *Medals for Dishonor*. New York: Willard Gallery, 1940. Exhibition catalogue.

Carandente, Giovanni. *Voltron*. Philadelphia: Institute of Contemporary Art, University of Pennsylvania, 1964.

Cone, Jane Harrison. *David Smith, 1906–1965*. Cambridge, Mass.: Fogg Art Museum, 1966. Exhibition catalogue.

Dehner, Dorothy. "Medals for Dishonor—The Fifteen Medallions of David Smith." *Art Journal* 37 (Winter 1977–78):144–50.

de Kooning, Elaine. "David Smith Makes a Sculpture." *Art News* 50, no. 5 (September 1951):38–41, 50–51.

Fry, Edward. *David Smith*. New York: Solomon R. Guggenheim Museum, 1969. Exhibition catalogue.

Geist, Sidney. "Prelude: The 1930s." *Arts* 30 (September 1956):49–55.

Greenberg, Clement. "David Smith." *Art in America* 43 (Winter 1956):30–33, 66.

_____. *David Smith: Sculpture and Drawings*. Philadelphia: Institute of Contemporary Art, University of Pennsylvania, 1964. Exhibition catalogue.

Hess, Thomas B. "Notes from Utopia." *Art News* 59, no. 3 (May 1960):23.

Hunter, Sam. *David Smith*. New York: Museum of Modern Art, 1957. Exhibition catalogue.

"The Irascible Eighteen." *New York Herald Tribune*, May 23, 1950, n.p.

"J. Gonzalez." *Cahiers d'art* 10 (1935):32–33.

Kramer, Hilton. "David Smith: Stencils for Sculpture." *Art in America* 50, no. 4 (Winter 1962): 32–43.

Krauss, Rosalind. *David Smith: Small Sculptures of the Mid-Forties*. New York: Marlborough-Gerson Gallery, 1968. Exhibition catalogue.

_____. *Terminal Iron Works: The Sculpture of David Smith*. Cambridge, Mass.: MIT Press, 1971.

_____. *The Sculpture of David Smith: A Catalogue Raisonné*. New York: Garland, 1977.

Lynes, Russell. *Good Old Modern*. New York: Atheneum, 1973.

McCausland, Elizabeth. Interview with David Smith. *Springfield [Mass.] Union and Republican*, November 10, 1940.

SELECTED BIBLIOGRAPHY

McCoy, Garnett, ed. *David Smith*. New York: Praeger, 1973.

McKinzie, Richard. *The New Deal for Artists*. Princeton: Princeton University Press, 1973.

Motherwell, Robert, and Ad Reinhardt, eds. *Modern Artists in America*. New York: Wittenborn, Schultz, 1949–50.

O'Connor, Francis V., ed. *Art for the Millions: Essays from the 1930s by Artists and Administrators of the WPA Federal Art Project*. Greenwich, Conn.: New York Graphic Society, 1973.

"Sculptor Rejects Award of $1,000." *New York Times*, November 1, 1961, p. 34.

Watson, Ernest. "From Studio to Forge: An Interview." *American Artist* 4, no. 3 (March 1940): 20–22, 31.

Withers, Josephine. "The Artistic Collaboration of Pablo Picasso and Julio Gonzalez." *Art Journal* 35, no. 2 (Winter 1975–76):107–14.

Zervos, Christian. "Picasso à Dinard, été 1928." *Cahiers d'art* 4 (1929):5, 6, 8, 11.

———. "Projets de Picasso pour un monument." *Cahiers d'art* 4 (1929):342, 344.

WRITINGS AND SPEECHES BY DAVID SMITH

Medals for Dishonor. New York: Willard Gallery, 1940. Exhibition catalogue.

"Open Letter to Roland I. Redmond, President of the Metropolitan Museum of Art." May 20, 1950. Signed by eighteen painters and ten sculptors, including David Smith. Mimeo.

Speech at Newcomb College, New Orleans, La., March 21, 1951.

Speech at Portland Museum of Art, Portland, Ore., March 23, 1952.

"The Sculptor and His Problems." Woodstock conference, Woodstock, N.Y., August 23, 1952.

Speech on radio station WNYC, New York, December 30, 1952.

David Smith. New York: Willard Gallery, 1954. Exhibition catalogue.

Letter to the Editor. *Art News* 55, no. 2 (April 1956):7.

Letter to the Editor. *Arts* 34, no. 9 (June 1960):5.

Letter to the Editor. *Art News* 59, no. 4 (Summer 1960):5.

"The Secret Letter." Interview with Thomas B. Hess in *David Smith*. New York: Marlborough-Gerson Gallery, 1964. Exhibition catalogue.

"Memories to Myself." Archives of American Art Quarterly *Journal* 8, no. 2 (April 1968):10–16.

Cleve Gray, ed. *David Smith by David Smith*. New York: Holt, Rinehart & Winston, 1968.

"Notes for 'David Smith Makes a Sculpture.'" *Art News* 68 (January 1969):35–38.

SELECTED UNPUBLISHED MATERIAL

American Federation of Arts, New York, Sara Roby Foundation file. Museum of Art, Carnegie Institute of Technology, Pittsburgh, Pa. Correspondence with David Smith, October 21, 1960–March 5, 1961.

Archives of American Art: George Biddle, Giovanni Carandente, Dorothy Dehner, Everett Ellin, Clement Greenberg, Robert Laurent, Edgar Levy, Lucille Corcos Levy, David Smith, and Marian Willard files.

Krauss, Rosalind. "The Sculpture of David Smith." Ph.D. dissertation, Harvard University, 1969.

Marcus, Stanley. "The Working Methods of David Smith." Ed.D. dissertation, Teachers College of Columbia University, 1972.

INDEX

Library of Congress Cataloging in Publication Data

Marcus, Stanley E., 1926–
   David Smith, the sculptor and his work.

   Bibliography: p.
   Includes index.
   1. Smith, David, 1906–1965. I. Title
NB237.S567M27 1983   730′.92′4   83–45148
ISBN 0–8014–1510–1